The Stripper's Guide
to Canoe-building

by David Hazen

TAMAL VISTA PUBLICATIONS
547 Howard Street
San Francisco, California 94105

My thanks go out to Kathi deFremery, who
not only provided full-time support services
to her family, but also assisted me greatly
in cleaning up my verbiage so that the novice
can wade through my book with much greater
dispatch. She also assisted me in the
reassembly of all the pieces in the right
order after the corrections were made, provided me with the space in her dining room
to do the layout and kept me going with
sandwiches, chili, beer, and cookies.

Thank you, Jack Davis, for permission to
reprint your article on how to make a canoe
paddle.

TAMAL VISTA PUBLICATIONS
547 Howard Street
San Francisco, California 94105

ISBN: 0-917436-00-8
Library of Congress Catalog Card Number: 76-19972

Dedication

To my lover, Barbara, for her devoted
tolerance, support, and space she has given
me to create, grow, and mature. For her
service to me as critic, soundingboard,
housekeeper, child supporter, and as a
beautiful inspiration for my love of life I
give deep and heartfelt thanks.

—David

Contents

Why a Strip Canoe?

Why a Strip Canoe?

So now that you're convinced that you want to build a canoe, you might wonder why, of all the types of canoes there are, should I choose to build a strip canoe?

Probably the first reason that you should consider is that you have all the skills necessary to be successful at building this type of boat. You don't have to be an expert at anything. You don't have to be a carpenter, experienced with fiberglass or super knowledgeable about boats. With desire, patience and the information in this book you've got all you need to get the job done bar a few strips of wood, some fiberglass and some hardware.

There are other advantages to wood strip canoes — whether you build it yourself or have it made. The laminated wood-strip and fiberglass construction produces a boat very high in strength and yet quite light. If you've ever loaded a canoe onto a car, or portaged it across shallow water, or packed it into an off-the-road lake, you'll know how nice it is to have a light boat. Yet you still have the comfort of knowing your boat will hang together in rough water.

To me, however, the most attractive thing about a strip canoe is still its beauty; its sleek lines and the natural beauty of the wood. To create something that is pleasing to look at and fun to handle brings a satisfaction that is long lasting.

The strip canoe combines beauty with great strength and light weight.

First-time Boatbuilder's Pep Talk

The issue that almost invariably comes up for everyone considering the construction of his own canoe is, "I don't think that I can build a beautiful boat like that." I would agree with you and go on to show you how that attitude is looking at the holes and not looking at the cheese. It is the attitude that I was stuck in during most of my career as a boatbuilder. It is the attitude which created a lot of unnecessary problems during the construction of some seventy boats.

The cheese that I want you to get out of using this book to build your own boat is NOT the boat. I don't care whether the boat you build comes out looking gross and ugly or light and beautiful. This book is about achieving a certain technical result, and I know that if you pay attention to the result and ignore the awareness of how you are doing it—the awareness of your feelings, attitudes, sensations, and memories—the result will be sterile.

The cheese that I want you to get is the experience. Just notice, and accept, what happens to yourself when you follow the directions. When I am in this head-space, I am not building the canoe, the canoe is building me. I am building the boat for the sake of discovering myself.

I want to share with you some of the things I have discovered, because you and I as human beings are faced with pretty much the same difficulties. What I say may not make the job of building the boat any easier for you, but if you get what I am saying, you might remember WHY you are building a boat when things are looking grim.

The first thing I want to tell you is DO IT. This book is not the experience; you have to create that. It is not the whole truth; it is only a map containing symbols for the reality which is in the process and in you. Allow the boat to come out of you the way it wants to come out, not the way you think it is supposed to come out. The way things are supposed to be is not the way things ARE. The fantasy I have in my mind of the boat I might build does not, will not, look like the boat I will actually build. I guarantee you that.

It will be pointed at both ends and it will float, all right, but all the events and contingencies that occur during the process of building are going to keep changing what the boat finally looks like. The finished boat is in you, in your body. You can't see it, visualize it, imagine it, until it happens. OK? You cannot imagine the grain structure of the interior of a board or tree; you can only see it after it has been cut open.

This book is only telling you how to operate a saw, not how to grow a tree. The tree is given. Cut it open, make little strips, glue them together, and so on. That is all. Just do it. See what happens. See yourself doing it.

To think about all the mistakes I've made and all the mistakes I might make is to guarantee that mistakes will be made. When whatever happens is whatever happens while doing a boat, then there are no mistakes; there are only surprises. It might mean I have to use a little plastic wood here and there, or inject a bubble in the fiberglass with some resin, or even peel off a layer of fiberglass that didn't adhere to the wood properly, but SO WHAT? It may even mean that I get bummed out, depressed, because I really wanted the boat to weigh less than 50 pounds, and it comes out 58, and there is nothing that I can do about it except build another boat. So what? A bummer is a bummer, and I'll get over it as soon as I decide that I'm either going to build another boat or not, so I might as well make that decision right now. You know? I have to remind myself not to mess around with the suffering, whipping myself for making mistakes. Perfect boats do not exist. The only question it makes sense to ask is, "What's next?"

It may be that what is next is an expression of anger. One of the greatest frustrations I had as a boatbuilder was being unable to allow myself the satisfaction of releasing my pent-up aggressions on the boat, with a chain-saw, ax, or torch. When I was in a bummer, I stayed away from the shop, did something else. I finally found myself out in the woods with a chainsaw, thinning trees with a forest service contractor, who called it "rape and maim" because he was so fond of the trees. I got into hating the trees sometimes if they would not fall in the direction I wanted them to. I shrieked curses at them insanely like a cornered cat. I would place myself in the path of a falling 30-foot, 4-inch diameter spruce or hemlock. Before it had gotten more than 5 or 10 degrees off vertical I'd throw the tree in the opposite direction. I don't know how much the trees weighed, but I know I couldn't have done it without all the adrenalin from the anger.

Well, a lot of the anger came from anger at myself for all the mistakes I thought I had made on the boats I had been building. Soon after that release I realized that not one of my customers ever saw those mistakes. They were usually too overwhelmed by the charisma of the boat and ignorant of what small details composed the multitude of "mistakes" that went into every boat. The irregularities actually contributed to the charm of the whole thing, because they meant that it was made by a human being and not a machine, which has some value in our day. However, I got the mistakes down to such an unnoticeable level that many observers doubted that I had actually made the boat with my own two hands, which was rather disappointing to me.

There's a successful boatbuilder within everyone.

I have also realized that the customer was not only buying the boat, he was also buying me, saying yes to me. I made a lot of friends out of customers, and non-customers who liked me because I was a boatbuilder. Sometimes it seemed like I had something special, a quality to my personality which contributed to my success as a boatbuilder. I don't deny that, but I vehemently deny that I am different from anybody else.

Everybody has a successful boatbuilder within himself, and by sharing with you the techniques and procedures I have developed from my experience, I offer to share with you some of that success. To receive it you must be willing to give the process your full attention and accept the fact that the boat does not represent you or your success or lack of it. What you learn about yourself will not be visible at all in the boat and may only manifest itself in that big grin of satisfaction on your face.

I want to thank you for making it possible for me to complete an important experience in my life, by sharing it. I built canoes and kayaks for four years, and I quit when I got too lonesome and the work held no more surprises. I found myself exploring in my mind more and more subtle aspects of boatbuilding which were meaningless to anyone except another boatbuilder. Writing has become my way of helping myself make sense about what I am doing. In the process of writing I create you, an empathetic boatbuilder, to listen to me express my reality. Inasmuch as it makes sense to you, you become me, I become you, and the stuff I am talking about is real. If it doesn't make sense to you, then I am talking about garbage that is unreal.

If you feel like sharing your reality with me, or confirming our mutual experience, I would love to hear about it. Sometimes very useful information pops up that way and contributes to further refinements in the content of this book. There is a feedback information page in the rear of this book.

You are now a graduate of the Boatbuilder's Pep Talk, a prerequisite to the reading of the rest of this book. If you don't have a "yes" feeling within you now, you'd better consider that the rest of this book is going to be hard to swallow, because I wrote it, and you've already spent several minutes with me. If you can feel a spark of enthusiasm, then I just made you into a boatbuilder, and the rest of the book will be all downhill.

Consider Design

With the drawings that accompany this book it is possible to build nine different hull shapes and, with slight modification, many more. You could also use the drawings as a starting point for designing your own boat. While you consider the possibilities of observing the ducks or surfing on the bow waves of a tug, consider also which of the hull shapes will best do the job efficiently and safely. Some hulls are specialized, but most hulls are a compromise somewhere between the range of extremes, in an attempt to achieve versatile performance.

Hull Shape Factors

By looking at how different hull shapes contribute to particular performance characteristics, you may then begin to combine certain hull-shape features into the compromise to suit your needs.

For **speed**, choose a long narrow hull with a bottom that is semi-circular from the end view. It should have a flat keel line (no "rocker") and a fine taper towards the ends, with little or no concave curvature in that taper. The boat should be rigid. Rowing shells are the epitome of this characteristic.

For **tracking** (ease in holding to a straight course), pick the above speed characteristics and add a keel to resist turning and low ends to avoid catching side winds. The Abenaki and Tsunami are specialized for speed and tracking.

For **stability**, choose a wide beam at the waterline, flat bottom, and full, blunt ends rather than narrowly-tapered ends. However, a broad bottom will pitch and roll more in wavy conditions than a round bottom. An alternative is to install the seats low, or kneel.

For **maneuverability**, choose a short, wide boat, with no keel, blunt ends, and a rockered keel line. Stability and maneuverability go together and tend to exclude speed and tracking, although compromises are possible.

For **displacement**, or high volume, which means the boat can carry heavy loads, choose a wide waterline, high sides, and a longer length.

For **seaworthiness**, the ability to handle waves and rough water, pick a boat with high displacement and add tumble-home (narrower at gunnels than at bilge), extra depth, and a spray-cover. Right behind the stem the hull should look like an inverted gothic arch, or a rounded vee, in order to throw waves outwards.

For **low weight**, choose a boat design with minimal surface area, such as the Abenaki, and, if possible, sacrifice some height on the ends, some depth in the middle. Use spruce, fir, or some other softwood for the gunnels instead of ash. Use a lightweight finishing cloth on at least the last exterior coat of glass, so that only two coats of resin are needed to fill its texture. I used 4 oz. cloth this way over a half-layer of 6 oz. to maintain some durability and made an 18' x 34" Micmac that weighed 48 lbs. I used cedar, which will make a boat 2 to 5 pounds lighter than spruce. I could have used 4 oz. cloth on the whole boat, but I thought it would be too fragile for canoe-camping.

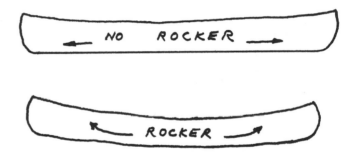

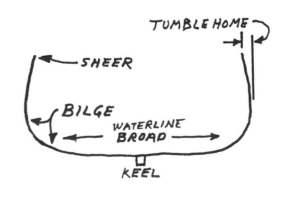

For **durability**, use 1/4" thick spruce instead of 3/16" thick cedar. Also, use 9 oz. cloth for the half-layers, or for all layers of the fiberglass layup. There is also available on the market an expensive epoxy resin which soaks deeply into the pores of the wood and is very tough. It is in two parts, hardener and resin, which are mixed 1:4. It may actually save

weight, since it reduces the need for cloth and therefore any great thickness of resin, which is where the weight is. The next best thing is probably a flexible polyester designed for poured flooring or furniture castings. It is almost impossible to crack it. This is most useful on the exterior of the canoe. Almost any fiberglassing resin can be used on the interior, where the criterion for durability is that the laminate not exceed its surface tensile strength and rupture inwards.

I am asked many times how well my boats withstand the punishment of shooting rapids. I am sure the answer lies with where your values are. The boat **can** be damaged under sufficient pressure and, in general, is comparable in strength to molded fiberglass boats weighing 10 to 20 pounds more. Round rocks will generally slide on, leaving only a scratch, or, under heavy impact, a bruise in the wood. It takes a hell of a whop with round rocks to rupture the hull inwards. The boat has to be moving rather fast with weight in it to do that.

I should mention here that the overall compression strength of the hull to massive forces, such as rolling in the surf, is poor. The thwarts and seats tend to be driven through the gunnels and hull.

Sharp-edged rocks are a bitch, because they cut the outside fiberglass rather easily, and the repairs are time-consuming. In severe cases, the rocks will remove large gouges of wood.

Now, all scratches in the bottom's resin look rather messy, aesthetically, and it is easy for me to judge myself as being careless. However, accidents do happen, and sometimes I want to shoot rapids more than I want to avoid the necessity for repairs or cosmetics. Right now I have two canoes, both Micmacs. One is 16' x 34" for whitewater, weighing 60 lbs.; the other is 18' x 34" for camping and cruising and weighs 48 lbs. Both have withstood round-rock abuse, but I would prefer not to expose them continually to that. I am now considering the purchase of a molded glass or ABS whitewater canoe with cockpits, which I may abuse without as much worry or guilt.

Glossary

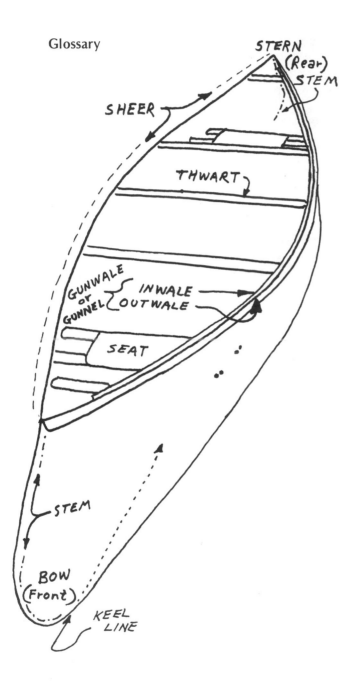

Construction Diagram

1 Spruce, cedar, or redwood strips, assembled over a jig with glue and staples, sanded, and sealed with lacquer.

2, 3 One and a half layers of fiberglass cloth in resin. High tensile strength glass skin over a relatively non-compressible core provides high strength-weight ratio.

4 Flexible isothalic polyester resin to absorb impact without cracking. Cover coats fill the weave of the glass cloth, making it invisible.

5, 6 Fiberglass cloth, one and a half layers, with coarse-textured finish.

7 Outwhale of ash, oak, spruce, or fir.

8 Inwale, fastened through hull to outwale with brass screws. Varnished.

9 Short thwart (instead of deck) of 1¼" fir dowel, fastened through gunnel with long brass screws.

10 Air chamber displaces 75 lbs. of water.

11 Seat fabric, grommeted and laced underneath the seat bars.

12 Stem, reinforced with extra layers of glass.

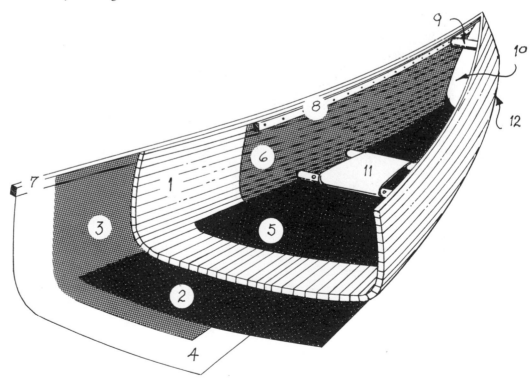

20' Micmac and 16' Micmac on snow

Micmac hull shape

The Micmac

The Micmac model is a popular recreational canoe. It has a broad beam for stability, buoyancy, and maneuverability. However, it is 2'' narrower than most other recreational canoes and thus easier to paddle. The slightly rounded bottom and narrowly tapered ends also contribute to its speed, thereby saving muscle energy. The Micmac has a slight rocker (upward curving keel line) for maneuverability, yet the stems are designed to assist in straight-ahead tracking. I suggest you try paddling it without a keel under a variety of conditions before deciding to add a keel. Compared to the classic circular stem shape, the sturgeon-nose stem has less crosswind-catching area and more water-catching area. The bow is designed to side-slip more than the stern to counteract the natural tendency of the canoe to turn away from the side on which the stern man is paddling. This produces a condition called "understeer," which is desirable for straight tracking, and which most manufacturers produce by shifting the seats sternward, causing the stern to squat lower, slowing the boat down.

The sheer line of the gunnels on the Micmac is almost an arc of a circle, producing depths of 19'' at the ends and 13'' in the middle. This has been shown by old-time canoe hero Calvin Rutstrum to be the best curve for fending off waves. The low ends, contrary to popular belief among white men, were more typical of Indian canoes than high ends, for a good reason: wind!

Canoes are very versatile. The use of each boat is often more limited by the skill and strength of the canoeist than by the design of the hull shape. However, the length of the boat and its underwater shape will allow it to do some things better than others. The 16' Micmac is best suited for exploring small rivers and shooting rapids, because its short length gives it maneuverability, and its blunt nose will rise in waves. The 17' Micmac is the sweet, sleek, all-purpose canoe and will shoot rapids and take long trips equally well. The 18' Micmac with 34'' beam qualifies for the cruising class in many races and makes a very sleek boat, whereas with a 36'' beam it becomes a load-carrying boat for long expeditions and ocean travel. The 20' Micmac is an enormous canoe, for crews of four or more going moose hunting.

Displacements are the weights which allow a 6" freeboard. Boat weights are for boats constructed with 6 oz. cloth and Western Red Cedar.

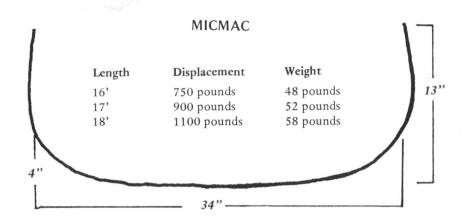

MICMAC

Length	Displacement	Weight
16'	750 pounds	48 pounds
17'	900 pounds	52 pounds
18'	1100 pounds	58 pounds

13"

4"

34"

The Abenaki

The Abenaki model is a fast cruising canoe. It was designed for marathon canoe racing. It has a narrow waterline beam, round bottom, and no rocker, which specialize it for speed and tracking. Only experienced canoeists should attempt to shoot rapids with it because of its limited maneuverability and tendency to knife through waves. The 18' model is a great choice for long-distance trips, and the 16' model makes a fine solo canoe, as well as a sport boat for two. It can also be made in a 14' version, for solo canoeing only, where portability is a major concern. The Abenaki hull is not as stable a platform as the Micmac hull, but this should be no problem to one who canoes frequently and is able to adapt to it.

Abenaki hull shape

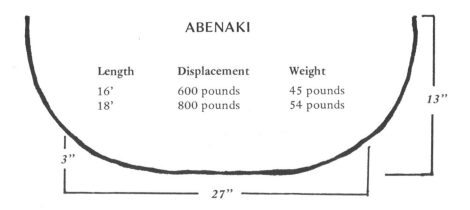

ABENAKI

Length	Displacement	Weight
16'	600 pounds	45 pounds
18'	800 pounds	54 pounds

13"

3"

27"

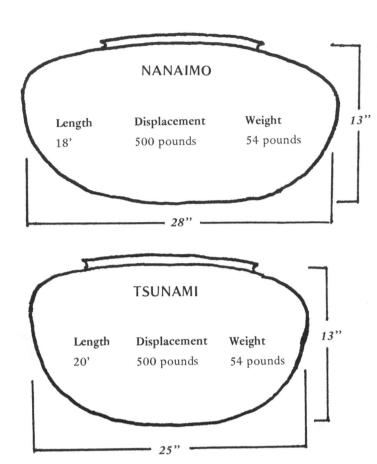

NANAIMO

Length	Displacement	Weight
18'	500 pounds	54 pounds

13"

28"

TSUNAMI

Length	Displacement	Weight
20'	500 pounds	54 pounds

13"

25"

Kayaks

Kayaks do require more care and skill than canoes. The two-man touring models, Nanaimo and Tsunami, are virtually impossible to empty of water without the assistance of solid ground, another boat, or possibly a bailing bucket. Re-entry from the water is a high art, and the same goes for two people trying to coordinate their struggles to do an Eskimo roll. However, they are fast! Also, once a paddler gains a solid grounding of experience, kayaks are much safer than canoes in rough water. Both the Nanaimo and Tsunami are designed for use on large bodies of water, such as the Columbia River, Puget Sound, and the ocean.

Kayaks are a totally different experience than canoes. A kayak is a personal wrap-around boat that puts the seat of your sensations right down into the waves, much like a sports car puts you onto the road. More of your body gets involved with the paddling and control of the boat than in a canoe. Your hips, legs, feet, and torso are used constantly. They are not easy to portage because there is no convenient place to balance them on your shoulders, and access to gear up in the ends of the boat is difficult.

The Nanaimo is about as wide as a kayak can go and still deserve the name. It is a stable recreational kayak with lots of room for gear. It has no rocker, to assist in tracking. The Tsunami is a speedy long-distance runner for the serious paddler. A customer-friend who lives near walrus and sea lions wrote to me, "Something inside of me goes WHEEE! when I lower myself into the cockpit." He also likes to play log-hockey with his boat when I visit him. The Tsunami can be made as designed, for two people, or it can be made 4' shorter by omitting the front cockpit.

Paddling through surf is difficult. The Tsunami's length needs two people to control it.

Sixteen-foot Abenaki

Safety vs. Efficiency

Sometimes it seems more relevant to ask how dangerous the canoeist is, rather than how dangerous the canoe. Are you accident-prone? My philosophy in designing or choosing a canoe is to select the features which will prevent total disaster (even the most experienced canoeist turns over when he least expects it) without sacrificing the performance of the boat. Canoes that are over-designed for stability tend to gurgle through the water, rather than slip. Skillful paddlers **cannot** overcome the built-in clumsiness and drag of a tub, but amateur paddlers **can** learn to control a sleek, sensitive boat with safety and stability. Thus, my boats demand some skill and common sense from their occupants. The Micmac and Nanaimo (kayak), of course, demand only a moderate amount of skill, whereas the Abenaki and Tsunami (kayak) demand a bit more. Anyone who bothers to develop his or her boating ability will be richly rewarded.

18' Micmac, 18' Abenaki, 20' Tsunami

Design Modifications

Any of the drawings accompanying this book may be modified to suit your particular needs. Read the section on building a jig first so that you can understand the language of this section.

The length may be easily changed after the forms are cut out of plywood and are ready for mounting on the strongback. Mount the center form and the stem forms first, and then fill in the space between with the remaining forms. To maintain some sleekness to the tapering ends, move the forms closest to the stems a proportionately greater distance from their normal locations. This amounts to adding or subtracting the length from the ends of the boat rather than the middle. However, some length can be removed or added to the middle as well. The best way to check the taper that results is to set up the forms on one half of the strongback in the locations chosen by preliminary calculations. Then staple temporary strips to the forms about 4" to 6" apart. Eyeball the curve the strip makes and move the forms forward or backward until the curve looks the way you want it. On the 17' Micmac it is almost a straight line from the stem to the number 3 form.

To change the width, trace the paper pattern onto the plywood with a gap centered on either side of the centerline of the form. The gap should be greatest on the center form and gradually diminish toward the ends. The edge of the form can be filled in over the gap with a French curve, or even freehand.

To change the rocker, change the height of the forms. Check the shape with temporary strips so that you don't get any weird bulges in the boat. The depth of the boat may be increased by simply extending the line of the forms.

To modify the curvature of the bottom, begin with the center form and gradually diminish the amount of alteration as you approach the stems. Check the shape with temporary strips. This work can often be done after some of the forms are set up, using shims on the edges of the forms to increase dimensions, or using a disc sander with 36-grit to decrease the shape.

To make a one-man kayak, eliminate the #4 and #5 forms and make the distance from #3 to #6 forms the same as from #6 to #7. The strongback will need to be 40" to 48" shorter.

Original Design

To begin completely from scratch, decide on the length, width, depth, and amount of rocker. Draw the center and stem forms, cut them out, and set them up on the strongback. Tack on a bunch of temporary strips. If the boat is to be symmetrical fore and aft, this only needs to be done for 1/4 of the boat, as the rest of the boat will be a mirror image of that quarter. Fill in the shape of the jig between the stem and center by trial-and-error fitting of forms, perhaps using cardboard at first. Cut it oversize and gradually cut it down to fit the strips, or until it pushes the strips into the curve you want. Try to get the forms about 18" apart, and never more than 24" apart. I like this method because I can see the boat in three dimensions and modify it instantly. There is another method, called lofting, used by naval architects, but it is done in two dimensions, and I believe it's too much trouble for me to learn how to do it.

dimensions given are examples only

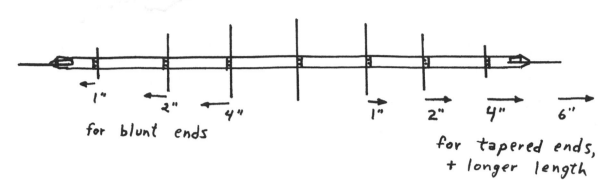

1"

2"

4"

1"

2"

4"

6"

for blunt ends

for tapered ends,
+ longer length

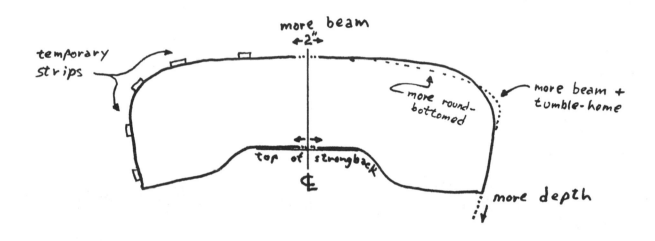

more beam

←2"→

temporary
strips

more round-
bottomed

more beam +
tumble-home

top of strongback

more depth

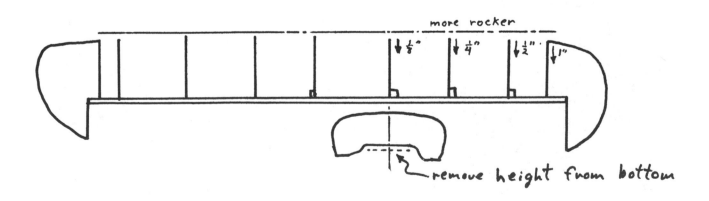

more rocker

↓⅛" ↓¼" ↓½" ↓1"

remove height from bottom

Find a Place

First of all, your building place must be warm and dry. High humidity will often prevent polyester resins from performing properly, particularly if the temperature suddenly drops, forming a condensate on freshly-applied resin. Humidity in the wood will do you no good either, for the resin will not gel over humid wood. Most glues and resins are formulated to give peak performance at room temperature, 70° F. Warmer temperatures do not generally hurt their performance, but simply shortens their pot life, or the time within which you can still work with them in a liquid state. Colder temperatures mean longer curing times, sometimes even stopping the cure altogether.

Secondly, ventilation is a must for the removal of harmful vapors and dusts. A large box window fan will do the job nicely, and it is better to have it suck air out rather than blowing air and dust onto your work. Place it low near the floor when working with resin, since the styrene monomer gases are heavier than air and tend to sink.

Good lighting is a requirement for operating power tools safely, squeezing air bubbles out of clear resin, and generally being able to see what you're doing without fatigue. A clip-on spotlight is very handy for portable intense lighting of local situations, such as when sanding and working inside ends of canoes and kayaks.

It is important that the work area be sealed off from living quarters when these are in close proximity. Noise, dust, and yucky smells are not nice to live with. Dust can often be contained with a large plastic drop cloth stapled to the ceiling along one edge, as a curtain.

Finally, provide yourself with a means for extinguishing a fire. Acetone, resin, styrene, and wood dust are all highly inflammable.

A warm, dry, well lighted place to work

Prepare Materials and Tools

If there were only one way to make a strip boat, and only one kind of boat to make, a shopping list would be easy. However, there are probably as many ways to build boats as there are people who build them. The choices between this material and that, or one tool and another, are complex. **The best way to plan your work is to understand the entire text of the instructions.** I have set in **bold type** materials as they appear in the context of their use. The checklist presented here is to give you a general idea of what is involved and is not intended to be a shopping list.

Orbital sander being used with goggles and respirator

Materials:

masking tape
string
nails: brads, 6d, 10d
spray paint
about 40 bf of :
  cedar, spruce, or redwood
hot water
rag

fiberglass cloth
catalyst
1 gallon acetone OR ammonia
roller covers

screws
nylon webbing
grommets
1¼" dowel
glass rovings
paper towels
varnish, sealer
scrap lumber
finished grade 2x6's
plywood
500 + 9/16" staples
1000 + ¼' staples
5 lbs. urea formaldehyde plastic resin
  glue OR 2 quarts white glue
3 gallons polyester resin for canoes
  16 to 18 feet
old newspapers
tracing paper
sandpaper
lag bolts
finish washers
acrylic canvas
½" dowel
ash or oak gunnels

Tools:

hammer	saw
drill, bits	square
wrench	level
plane	bandsaw, jigsaw, sabre-
rasp or surform	saw, or coping saw
paintbrushes,	screwdriver
natural bristle	staple gun
paint roller handle	utility knife
table saw (optional)	sidecutter pliers
clothespins	scissors
disc, belt, or	ventilation fan
orbital sander	goggles
ear plugs	respirator
veterinary syringe	C-clamps
grommet setter	

Select the Wood

Western Red Cedar often has a beautiful variety to its color within each board, is the lightest wood for this purpose, and resists moisture penetration. However, the oils and lignins in it inhibit the cure of the polyester resin used for fiberglassing, and it must be sealed with lacquer. It is also very difficult to procure as of this writing.* Redwood has the same physical properties as Red Cedar; it is light and strong, and also needs to be sealed. It usually does not have the variety of color that Red Cedar has. Sitka Spruce is a very blond wood, uniform in color, denser and heavier than Cedar, but very strong. It does not need to be sealed. It can be stained with a transparent exterior stain before fiberglassing. It is very important, however, to test the adhesion of your particular resin to your particular stain on a sample of wood before attempting to do the whole boat!

I prefer Sitka Spruce because it is available, it is very strong, and the grain is usually quite straight and free of knots. About the only place in the USA that sells it is Fred Tebb and Sons, Inc., 1906 Marc St., Tacoma, Washington 98421, but try your local yard first. Wilderness Boats (address on p. 88) sells spruce already ripped into strips.

There are other woods which may be used for this purpose. I know that Philippine Mahogany has been used and usually results in a heavy boat. Pine would make a good strip boat if you could get it in clear boards 18' long or were willing to splice all your strips. Poplar is another possibility. Any species that produces long, knot-free planks with a reasonably straight, closely-spaced grain pattern and is reasonably light and strong will do.

The best boards have no humidity or oil in them. Kiln-dried (yes!) light-colored sap wood is best. Air-dried wood may have more "life" in it, but that virtue is somewhat obscured after it is sandwiched between two layers of non-stretch fiberglass, and it usually has more humidity in it than kiln-dried lumber. Humidity and polyester resin don't mix.

The boards should have slash grain, so that the strip has vertical grain when ripped from the edge. Wider boards have more slash grain

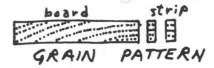

GRAIN PATTERN

and will produce more strips with less waste, but they cost more per board foot and are difficult to maneuver. The boards must be planed smooth to ¾" thickness. Avoid boards with a lot of knots, handling gouges, lengthwise splits, or planer skips. Sometimes boards are a little thicker in the last 6" from the ends, but this can be hand-planed off if you notice it.

Calculate the Quantity

In order to make a calculation of how many board feet you will need, first refer to the chart below to get the number of ¾" x ¼" strips that are needed for the particular model you want to build.

Model	Sides #—length	Bottom #—length	Tips #—length
18' x 36" Micmac	30 — 20' 8 — 18'	28 — 16'	8 — 16'
17' Micmac	32 — 18' 4 — 16'	24 — 16'	8 — 16'
16' Micmac	28 — 18' 8 — 16'	21 — 16'	8 — 16'
16' Abenaki	36 — 18'	20 — 16'	leftovers
20' Tsunami	62 — 20'	34 — 18'	none

*Western Red Cedar is available from Beaver Lumber Co. in Santa Clara, California.

The next step is to calculate how much board width is necessary to produce the number of strips you need. Using a saw with a kerf (the slot the saw chews out) of 1/16" to 3/32", you can get about 30, ¼" thick, strips from a 12" wide plank (finished to 11½") depending on how much is wasted because of knots, splits, or inaccurate ripping.

Now, to get the total board width of 16' lumber needed for a 17' Micmac, for example, the total number of 16' strips --36-- adds up to 9" of wood (36 strips x ¼") and about 3" of kerf (36 strips x 3/32"), or a total board width of 12". A board foot is 1" nominal thickness (finished to ¾") by 12" by 12". Therefore 16 board feet are needed for this example; 16' of 12" wide lumber that is 1" thick. You should buy boards that are 4" to 8" wide, however, not 12" widths. Less than 4" creates too much waste and more than 8" is too hard to handle in the saw. You should also buy a little more wood than you need to allow for waste.

So, for this example, when you arrive at the lumberyard you would specify 17 board feet of 1" S4S (surfaced four sides) by 16', random width, redwood (or whatever wood you choose), clear, dry, slash grain. Similar specifications are needed for the 18' strips needed to build the 17' Micmac.

Normally, I rip strips to 3/16" thickness, unless I am making a 20' Micmac or a boat that I want to be extra tough. For a 20' Micmac, I recommend 5/16" thick strips on the bottom and 1/4" thick strips on the sides. If you have doubts about your craftsmanship and don't mind a few extra pounds in your boat, use 1/4" thick strips in order to give yourself an extra margin of thickness. Without it, there is a possibility of sanding the boat dangerously thin in areas where there are tight curvatures.

Ripping the Boards

A bandsaw has a kerf of about 1/16", is relatively safe and easy to operate, consumes little power. However, the kerf is rough, which means more sanding and less wood remaining in the boat. The blade may wander as much as 1/16" from where you set it. Wide blades (1/2"+) will wander less than narrow ones. Use a new, sharp blade. Tightly clamp a long, straight fence to the table of the bandsaw. It helps to have a support for the middle of the board when it is at the very beginning and ends of the stroke through the saw, because 18' planks sag a lot. Bring the blade guide down close to the wood, and set all the running guides for the blade snugly. Use one person to hold the wood against the fence, the other to push and pull the plank.

A table saw will produce uniform thickness strips that have smooth faces. However, table saws make a lot of noise, consume a lot of power, throw sawdust in your eyes, demand that you take great care to avoid binding the blade with that 18' long lever, and at 3400 rpm can make mistakes in a flash. It is a powerful precision tool that must be treated with respect. Use a push-stick between your hands and the blade when fencing the board. When setting the fence, measure to both the front and the rear of the blade to make sure the fence is parallel to the blade. You could also clamp a board to the fence to extend its length and rig a support for the middle of the board. Two people and a one-horse saw motor are needed for this job, and three people would make it faster.

Generally, the smaller diameter saw blades are made of thinner gauge metal and thus will remove less wood from the board. A 6" planer blade that is hollow-ground will have a kerf of 1/16" to 3/32" and leave an extremely smooth kerf. It should be used with a blade lubricant, such as Simo-spray. The blade must be well-sharpened. For oily, abrasive woods like cedar and redwood, it may be better to use a 7¼" carbide-tipped blade made by Simmonds, which has a kerf of 3/32". Any ripping blade that has some set to its teeth will cause a rougher cut, but will also not bind or pick up pitch from the board.

When you are all set up to begin ripping, one person stands at the saw and gives some clearly-anticipated signals with his hands to direct the board up, down, left, right, forward, back, or stop. He also holds the board down and in

Ripping strips with a bandsaw

against the fence. The other person supplies all the forward push on the board. Push cautiously, focusing your attention on the edge of the board where it meets the fence and the noise of the motor. Don't allow a gap to appear between the board and the fence, and don't push so hard against the fence that you bind the blade and labor the motor. Breathe deeply and walk like a cat, holding the board away from your body. If you push with your gut, the board will swing sideways as you shift weight from one foot to the other. Because of the sag in the board, you may have to begin the push with the end of the board up under your nose.

When the board is about halfway through the saw, the pusher may either trot to the other end and begin pulling, or he can take over the fencing, and the fencer pulls. The latter arrangement makes it faster to walk the board back for another pass and allows each person to specialize in developing the knack for either pushing or pulling. When pulling, watch the kerf. It should neither spread apart nor close up after the saw blade. Grip the strip and the board. At the end of the pass leave the board on the saw table while you give the strip a little jerk off onto the floor.

I have been told that it is possible to rip strips with a portable circular saw ("Skilsaw"), but I have not tried it. The board is held stationary, the saw has a fence set at 1/4", and one walks along the board with the saw. For a minimal investment, it sounds like a workable idea. My experience, however, has been with bandsaw and tablesaw.

Select Fiberglass Cloth

To make a strong boat without weight, plan to use one full layer of cloth inside and out, and a half-layer covering the broad part of the bottom, underneath the full layer, inside and out. The sides of the boat need to be stiff enough to withstand cartopping, and the bottom should be strong enough to ride over a few submerged rocks or logs. I will mention here that it is possible to coat the exterior with epoxy resin with little or no glass cloth in it, perhaps saving weight, but I have no experience with this method.

For a medium-duty boat, for general recreation, I use a 6 oz. weight of fiberglass cloth. For a 20' Micmac, or any other boat to be used in rapids or rocky beaches, use a 9 oz. cloth in all layers. Where the weight of the boat is a primary consideration and the owner is willing and able to take extra care of the hull, a 4 oz. cloth may be used in all layers or only in the final exterior layer. The lower the weight of the cloth, the finer the weave and the lower the weight of resin it will soak up. Using a fine-weave cloth on the exterior of the boat means fewer covering coats of resin, fewer pounds of resin, are necessary.

To calculate the amount of cloth needed, measure the perimeter of the center form to get the width (60" wide cloth for most Micmacs). The length needed is 3 times the length of the boat (1½ layers on each side of the wood). It is all right to have seams if wide cloth is not available, but the extra resin needed to cover the seams adds weight.

Avoid polypropylene cloth. Used with clear resin, its texture will soon become visible after a few cycles of hot sun and cool-cold weather. Its adhesion and impact resistance was not noticeably better than glass in the tests that I made with it. For aesthetic purposes, glass is better for its invisibility over the wood. Dupont is manufacturing a new super-cloth for boat-building, Kevlar 49, but I don't know if it is as transparent as glass cloth. It is expensive.

Select the Resin

Polyester resin is a liquid plastic composed of a long-chain hydrocarbon molecule. It is suspended in a vehicle, or solvent, called a styrene monomer. It is transformed into a solid by heat, which causes the long-chain molecules to grow longer and interlock. The heat is produced by a chemical reaction between two compounds mixed into the resin, promoter and catalyst. Usually the promoter is already in the resin when you purchase it, is often a salt of cobalt, and colors the resin yellow, pink, blue or purple. Without it, resin is water-clear. The catalyst is also clear. It is a strong peroxide, and it is the oxidation of the promoter that causes heat. A little bit of catalyst goes a long way. The heat causes the resin to gel in about a half hour. It cures rapidly at first and then more slowly, reaching full

cure anywhere from a few days to a month later. Don't worry--it's 98% cured and ready to sand about 4 hours after gel time. Incidentally, it's not technically correct to say that a resin "dries". Evaporation of the solvent, styrene monomer, does occur but the plastic has to "cure" to get hard and tough.

Air actually inhibits the cure of polyester resin, and the surface of the resin will remain tacky unless it is sealed off from the air. If the manufacturer does not call the resin a "surfacing" resin or state that a surfacing agent or sanding agent has been added to it, this agent can be bought separately. The surfacing agent is paraffin, dissolved in styrene monomer at the rate of 1/4 lb. per gallon. The paraffin floats, or oozes, to the surface and seals off the air. It also prevents the next layer from bonding, unless the next layer is applied within 20 minutes of gel time or after curing and sanding.

The best polyester resin for the exterior of the boat is called flexible *isothalic* polyester. It is often designed for poured flooring or furniture castings, and is very tough, refusing to crack under impact. A standard laminating (bonding) resin is usually a rigid *orthothalic* resin which shatters on impact. This type of resin is suitable only for the interior of the boat. In fact, almost any polyester resin, rigid or flexible, with surfacing agent may be used on the interior. Some manufacturers market what they call a *surfboard* resin which is supposed to be clear, impact resistant, and have a surfacing agent and ultraviolet absorber mixed into it. This is an optimum combination of features.

A 16' to 18' canoe will need about three gallons of resin to laminate 6 oz. cloth. Allow two gallons for the exterior and one gallon for the interior. Larger boats or heavier cloth will need more; smaller boats, lighter cloth, less.

Epoxy resin is an alternative to polyester resin. There is available for $2.00 a description of Wood Epoxy Saturation Technique (WEST System) from Gougeon Brothers, 706 G Martin Street, Bay City, Michigan 48706. The strength to weight ratio is presumably higher for exterior coating than polyester fiberglass. The cost may be higher too.

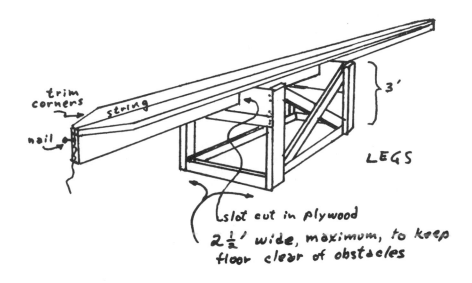

trim corners

string

nail

3'

LEGS

slot cut in plywood
2½' wide, maximum, to keep
floor clear of obstacles

Finished jig for 16' Abenaki

Make the Jig

A jig is made of two parts, a strongback and forms.

A strongback is the foundation of the jig, composed of a beam resting on legs. It must hold the forms firmly in a straight line, like a backbone holding ribs.

Strongback

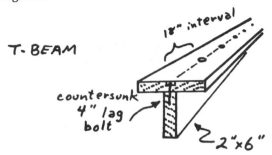

EITHER assemble the strongback from two 2" x 6" clear, dry finish grade **lumber**, picked for straightness, 2' shorter than the length of the intended boat. The stem will extend one foot beyond each end of the strongback. The strongback can be made 3' shorter than the boat if the stem forms extend 18" beyond the end of the strongback. This is sometimes useful if more than one boat of different lengths are to be made. Thus, a 16' and 17' canoe can be made using one 14' strongback. Assemble the two 2 x 6's into a T-beam using **4" lag bolts** at 18" intervals. Countersink the heads.

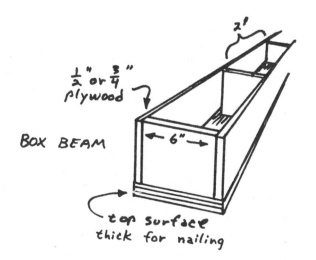

OR assemble the strongback from **plywood**, 1/2" or 3/4" thick, cut, glued, and nailed into an open box beam with internal bracing every 2 feet, and a double-layered top surface. The beam should measure 6" x 6" and be assembled on a perfectly flat floor in order to insure the flatness of the beam. Due to the difficulty of tapering the corners, make the beam 3' shorter than the canoe.

OR assemble the strongback from laminated **two-by-fours** or whatever materials are available. The strongback beam must be very rigid with a perfectly flat top surface. After the strongback is assembled, its top surface can be planed level, if there are no nails in the way.

If the strongback is only 2' shorter than the canoe, trim the corners to a tapering point. This will allow you to strip over this point and get the boat off the jig more readily.

Paint the beam with one coat of **sealer or varnish**, to prevent any swelling or warping.

Make legs for the strongback to keep it firm, steady, and level, using scrap **two-by-four lumber**. Design the legs so that the top of the strongback is about 3 feet from the floor, if you are a 6' high people. If you are something else, adjust it to your own height.

Using a level and shims under the legs, make the strongback level from end to end, and from side to side.

Tack a small **nail** into the approximate middle of each end of the strongback. Stretch a **string** along the top of the strongback from one nail to the other. **Spraypaint** the string with any dark color. Remove the string, leaving its silhouette as the centerline. A snapped chalkline is all right for bricklaying, but a canoe is not a brick. I stopped using snapped stringlines when I discovered a 1/2" error at the middle of the boat.

Begin at the center form, the middle of the boat, and measure off the positions of the forms along the centerline of the strongback. Draw a pencil line at a right angle to the centerline using a **square**. Write the number of the form that goes at each position.

LAYOUT

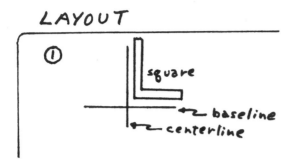

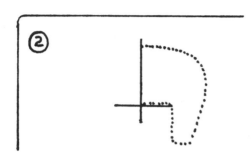

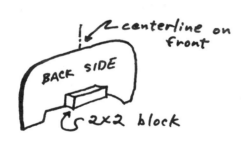

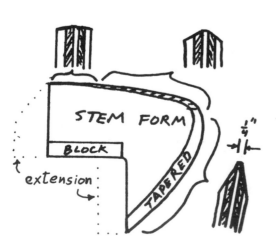

Forms

Make the forms, the temporary ribs of the boat, to hold its shape until it is fiberglassed. For most boats, you will need one 4' x 8' shop cutting panel of BD utility grade **plywood**, interior glue, sanded one side. Three-quarters inch thick is preferred but ½" will do. Two sheets are necessary for the 18' and 20' Micmac canoes.

Using a light table or a window, trace the shape of the stem form and air chamber bulkheads onto **tracing paper** from the newsprint drawings. After it has been traced, its length may be extended 6" to accommodate a strongback that is 3' shorter than the boat, by using a square. All the forms may be traced in order to preserve the drawings.

The simplest way of tracing the newsprint sheet drawings onto the plywood for cutting is to begin with the largest form, the center form, and cut its outline with **scissors**. With a carpenter's square, draw the centerline of the form and its horizontal baseline on the plywood's sanded side. Lay the paper pattern over these lines, and carefully trace along the edge of the paper. Make sure the paper lies completely flat and does not move. Repeat the the procedure for all the other forms, making two copies of each pattern on the plywood, one for the stern half of the boat, the other for the bow. Check for symmetry by folding the paper on its centerline.

If you have a **sabre-saw**, the forms can be cut directly out of the large sheet of plywood. Otherwise, cut between the forms with a **handsaw** so that individual forms can be trimmed on a **bandsaw**, **jigsaw**, or **coping saw**.

Use **sanding block**, **rasp**, or **surform tool** to smooth out the uneven squiggles along the edges of the forms.

Mount 2" x 2" **blocks** along the baseline of the forms, on the side opposite from the centerline. Use **glue** and **nails** or **screws**. This cleat must be flush-even with the baseline of the form, and at least 6" long. Mount a block along the side of the stem form.

Taper the stem form's leading edge as illustrated, using a rasp, plane, disc sander, or bandsaw.

Assembly

Attach the stem forms at each end of the strongback, so that the centerline of the form is directly over and in line with the centerline of the strongback. Use a level to check the stem form for vertical alignment. If the surface of the form is not vertical, use thin cardboard or wood **shims** along one edge to adjust its angle. The 2 x 2 cleats are now attached with **nails** or carriage bolts. **Carriage bolts** are much more expensive, but if used in slightly oversize holes, they allow for making fine adjustments, are easier than nails to remove, and extend the life of the cleats and strongback when more than one boat is made with the same forms. It is very difficult to pry the forms off the strongback from below when the forms are covered with the canoe, unless the stempiece and first form at one end (at least) are fastened with carriage bolts.

Stretch a taut string from the top of one stem form to the other. If there is no rocker to the boat, a nail in the center ply of the plywood can be used as a cinching-post for the string. If there is rocker, a piece of wood-strip stapled to the side of the stem form, extending above it in double thickness as illustrated, will do the job of keeping the string over the center of the strongback centerline.

Attach the forms to the strongback so that they are square to all three dimensions. Begin with the #1 form. Stand it up on the top of the strongback with its centerline facing the middle of the boat. The centerline of the form should be directly in line with the centerline of the strongback and the tautline. The chances are pretty good that it is off by a few degrees. If you are using nails, tack the form in position lightly with one nail in the center of the cleat. Make sure the bottom of the form's centerline is on the strongback centerline. Use shims to bring the top of the form's centerline under the tautline. Tolerate 1/32" of error when sighting this in from above.

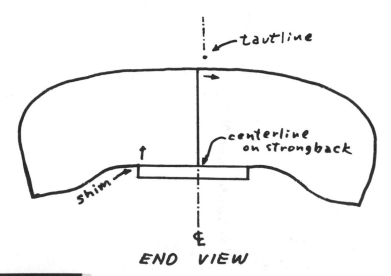

END VIEW

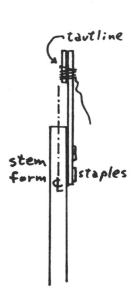

Box beam with stem forms and tautline

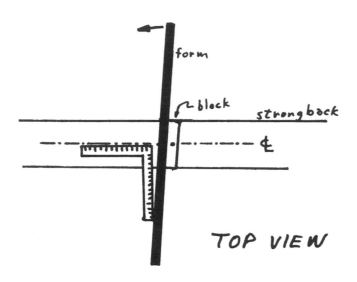

TOP VIEW

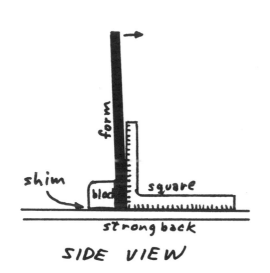

SIDE VIEW

When using carriage bolts, tighten them finger tight and loosen them to insert shims. Nails can be pried up a little to insert a shim, and then tapped down lightly to check the results.

Use shims to bring the form to vertical, a right angle with the top surface of the strongback. Tolerate 1 or 2 degrees error.

Adjust the form to a horizontal right angle with the centerline of the strongback. Tolerate 1 or 2 degrees error. Nail down firmly, or tighten carriage bolts. Double-check all alignments.

Repeat this process with the #2 form, and so on to the other end of the boat. Always place the cleat away from the middle of the boat, the centerline towards the middle.

Remove the tautline.

If there are blows in the plywood (gaps) showing along the edges of the forms, whittle small pieces of wood to plug the holes, gluing them in oversize and sawing off the excess after the glue dries. White glue is fine.

Cover all the edges of the forms with **masking tape**. On the stem form, cover all of the tapered area. Masking tape prevents glue and resin from sticking to the forms, making the canoe easy to remove.

Remember how the drawings looked? It was difficult to imagine how the canoe would look, what its shape was really like, all stretched out, from those stacked-up, two-dimensional drawings. Still, there was probably some feeling for the shape which you had. Now, looking at the jig, what are your feelings? Walk around the jig, judging the size and shape, the curves and lines of the boat that isn't there. Eyeball it from the end. Can you see it?

I had run the rapids in an egg-shell, as it were. Wondering men had looked at my Allegro, *and speculated on her voyage, and praised her beauty. I thought: "You admire only her comely form; but I love her lightsome mastery over waves, her free runs with the wind, her confiding intimacy with sea or lake, river or torrent, and with all this, her intrepid spirit, ready for any adventure, and her staunch friendship tried in flood and field, by night and by day.*

CHARLES H. FARNHAM, 1881

Assemble the Wood Over the Jig–Stripping

Mark Football Shape

Select a straight **strip** to lay on the keel line, the centerline of the forms, from the bow stem to the stern stem form. For most of the Micmacs, a 16' strip is the right length. Use **9/16" staples** to staple this strip to the forms, allowing it to hang out over the stem forms. Staple the strip to one stem form, then walk to the other end and pull the strip into a straight line, staple it, go to the middle form, staple the strip over the centerline there, and finish stapling to the other forms, continually checking the strip for straightness.

The bottom of the canoe is made of strips laid parallel to the keel strip and trimmed into the shape of a long, narrow football. The widest part of the football, of course, is at the center form. Measure the following distances outward from the centerline of the center form:

18' x 36" Micmac	14"
17' Micmac	13¼"
16' Micmac	12½"

For other boats not listed here, simply choose a point where the broad part of the bottom begins to turn sharply into the bilge, similar to the points indicated by the above measurements. Check the drawings to develop a feel for where the point should be.

Select one of your longer strips, and staple the middle of it to the center form, face down, with its edge against the mark for the width of the football. Use two or three staples.

Bring the end of the strip over to the base of the stem form where it meets the keel strip. Allow it to form a smooth, natural curve. Don't pull along its length. Staple it to the keel strip. Do the same to the other end, and eyeball the whole curve for symmetry. Mark a dark, heavy line on each form where this strip crosses the form. This curve approximates the trim line for the edge of the football.

Repeat this procedure for the opposite side of the boat. The apex of the football should be in the center of the keel strip.

For canoes being built with the Kootenay stems and using the flatter "stern" line from the plans, move the apex of the football 4" onto the stem of the stern. This prevents excessive curvature of the side strips.

Tape a 1/8" thick shim of cardboard or wood under the nose of the staple gun. This will prevent the staples from being driven entirely down, making them easy to pull out later.

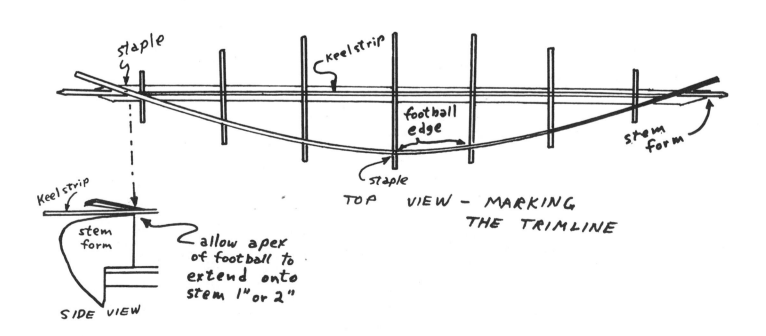

Gluing

Urea-formaldehyde glue comes as a tan powder that is mixed with cold water. It dries brittle, and is easily sanded with power tools. **White glue** will soften during the friction-heat of sanding and gum up the sandpaper. If you plan to hand-sand the boat, or use an orbital sander, white glue will do the job. It is not waterproof, of course, but once the boat is fiberglassed, the quality of the glue is trivial.

Aliphatic Resin Glue has the same general characteristics as white glue, except it dries harder, making it much easier to sand. Franklin's Titebond Glue is Aliphatic Resin and it may be in some hobby shops, but it is not very common. (Thank you to Leon Olson, Lompoc, California)

Mix the urea-formaldehyde glue with a tiny amount of water, and gradually add more and more until it is the consistency of pancake batter. Do not mix more than 6 to 8 fluid oz. of glue at one time, or you will not be able to use it up before the end of its pot life at 70° F.

Strip the Football

Lay 2 to 4 strips alongside the keel strip. Adjust their position lengthwise until one end is a few inches outside the trim line of the football and the other end has a surplus of strip. Break off the surplus strip a few inches outside the trim line. Save the short pieces in a pile somewhere.

Keeping the strips in the same relative order, **clamp** them face-to-face so their edges are exposed. Spring-operated welder's clamps are ideal for this. The strips may be placed on the floor if it is clean, or across the tops of the forms.

Apply glue to the edges of the strips. You may use a **brush** or **roller**. In either case, be generous enough so that glue oozes out of the joints when the strips are pressed into place.

Lay the strips back along the keel strip in the proper order, with the glued edges all facing the keel strip. Double-check the overhang at each end to make sure that it is over the trim line. Push the strips tightly together against the keel strip at the center form. Using 9/16'' staples, staple the strips to the center form. In the broad flat areas of the boat one staple can usually hold two strips in place, if it is shot in with one leg in each strip.

Staple the strips to the forms working towards one end and then the other, pressing the strips tightly together each time a staple is fired.

Near the ends of the boat, where the curvature is greater, one or more staples per strip may be necessary to force the strip to twist into the proper shape. Some strips may end in mid-air. Staple them to their neighbor, using a staple shot with one leg in each strip, as if you were sewing the boat together. In some cases it may be better to leave the strip extra long so that it can reach a form and be stapled to it.

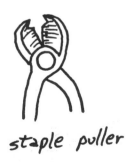

staple puller

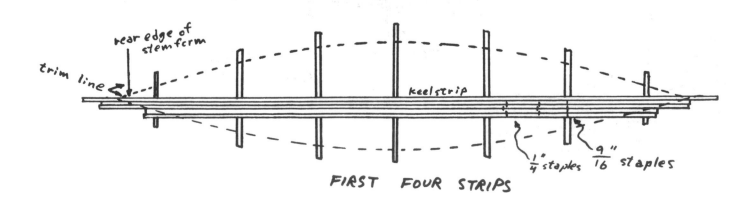

FIRST FOUR STRIPS

If you are having difficulty with strips springing away from the forms in the areas of tight curvature, try tilting the staple gun up on its nose so that the 9/16" staple goes in at an angle. If this doesn't work, use small wire **brads** (finishing nail).

Change the **staples** in the gun to **1/4" long**. Between each form across each glue line shoot one or two staples, or more if necessary, to hold the strips tightly together and in flush alignment. Feel the undersides of the strips for any edges that might be lower than others. Be careful not to staple the end of your finger. Squeeze the strips together each time a staple is shot.

Clean hands, staple gun, and the tops and bottoms of the strips with a **warm**, **damp rag** or **paper towel**. The glue may irritate your hands, especially if you have any scratches or cuts, and it is a lot easier to sand the boat if it doesn't have great globs of glue all over it. Also, clean the brush or roller frequently with hot water, or it will coagulate, gel, or just plain plug up.

Repeat the stripping process with shorter and shorter strips until the entire football area is covered. The last several pieces to be fitted, such as those 8' and shorter, will be the surplus pieces broken from longer strips already fitted into the bottom. Eyeball the trim line from time to time to see if there are any unusual dips or waves in it.

Extra glue which has thickened is perfect for rubbing into gaps between the strips with the fingers, in case there are places that didn't get enough glue or didn't get squeezed tightly enough.

Allow the glue to cure overnight at room temperature. If the temperature is below 60° F., the glue may be gummy in the morning and may never cure at all.

Trim the Football

Pull the staples out of the football, except for the staples outside of the trim line. A neat **staple-puller** can be made from a pair of wire-cutters. File or grind a small notch into the jaws immediately below their tips. Do not file the tip, or the staple will slip out. An office-type staple remover also works.

Measure and mark the width of the football at the center form. Repeat the procedures as outlined above for determining the trim line of the football with a long strip bent edgeways from bow to stern around the center

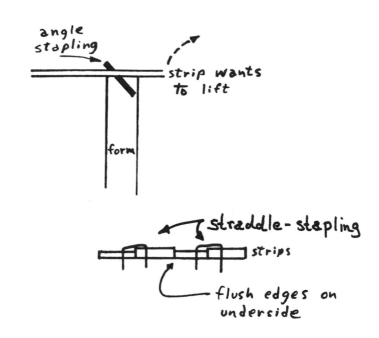

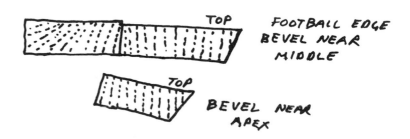

form. Draw a pencil line along the strip onto the boat's bottom where it is to be cut.

Cut along the line with a **sabre-saw**, **router**, or **knife**. Begin at the center form and cut towards the ends to minimize chipping and splitting the wood inside the football. Proceed cautiously, and do not cut inside the line. If using a sabre-saw, hold the nose of the saw down firmly to prevent chattering, and use a short blade. You will have to saw through the edge of the plywood station-forms. It does not hurt the form to have a slit in its edge.

Remove all the trimmings from the forms. The football is now loose from the jig. Slide it over to one side so that the edge is exposed. Use a **block-plane** to fair the edge into a smooth curve. Bevel the edge inwards at the bottom so that it will fit the first strip to be glued along its edge. Near the apex, increase the bevel to almost 45°. Be very critical of the fairness of the curve and the accuracy of the fit. Test the fit against a strip bent along its edge—look for gaps, and then shave down the high spots until it fits. Often the high spots are easiest to see when sighting along the edge.

The football piece may decide to slide off onto the floor while your back is turned. That would be a minor disaster if it happened, so be aware of its position at all times while planing its edge.

Staple the football to the forms in its original, correct position. A few staples in the middle and several along its edge are all that are needed.

Strip the Side

Begin at one edge of the football and strip the entire side of the jig. Use the floor as a place to glue the strips.

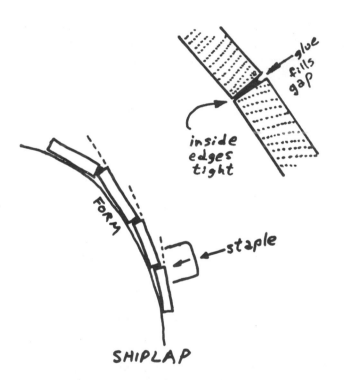

SHIPLAP

Pick up the first strip at its middle after glue has been applied to its edge. Press it into position against the edge of the football at the center form and staple it with a 9/16" staple. While holding the strip from falling, step sideways to the next form, lift and press the strip against the edge of the football, and staple it to the form. Continue to the stem form, stapling the strip to each form. Then return to the middle and repeat the operation towards the other end of the boat. The ends of the strips will overhang beyond the stem form.

Change to 1/4" staples. Many staples are needed along the edge of this first strip to sew it tightly to the football piece. Keep pressing it tight and stapling across the glue line until all the gaps are taken up.

Pick up the second strip, balancing it at its middle again, and as you center it on the center form, check to be sure you have enough strip to overhang each end of the boat. A coat-hanger wire bent into a hook at each end may be hung on the overhang of the first strip, to catch the sagging ends of the next strips. Use the 9/16" staples to staple to the forms, working from the center form towards the stems. In the bilge area, it helps to prevent ship-lap if these staples are shot in with one leg in each strip, straddling the glue line. In the flatter areas on the side, staples may be shot into the center of the strips. The strips in the bilge area are being twisted, so more 1/4" staples, driven in at an angle, straddling the glue line, are needed than in the flat areas. Remember to press the glue-joints tight, and to have a generous amount of glue.

Because the strips are lying over a curve, the inside edges should be tight together and the outside edges slightly apart. The inside edges should also be flush together. If stapling does not seem adequate to hold the strips down on the forms, use wire brads. Regularly clean off the glue from the wood, hands, staple gun, and roller or brush.

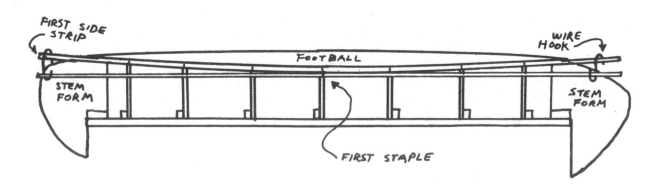

Continue stripping the full side of the boat. When you reach the bottom corner of the center form, apply the last full-length strip. For a kayak hull, there are no more strips; but for a canoe, the sheer line must be filled in with partial-length strips.

Strip the Tips

Lay a tape measure 8' long on the floor, with the zero end against a wall. The following series of partial-length strips will be needed to make a 19"-high Kootenay (sturgeon-nose) stem on the Micmac canoe: 82" 72" 63" 52" 42" 33" 25" 16" 12". On the 18' Micmac, an extra strip 96" long may be inserted for slightly higher ends.

Push a strip against the wall with its end next to the tape measure zero end. Break it off at the desired length, and repeat 4 times, so that you make 4 complete sets of partial-length strips, one for each "corner" of the canoe. If there are any partial-length strips left over from making the football, use them instead of breaking up more full-length strips.

If you are making a canoe with different height tips, or a different curvature to the stem, determine the length of the broken strips by holding the strip on the jig in its approximate position from the stem to just beyond the sheer trim line. Break it off, glue it into position, and repeat until the entire tip is covered. If the boat is to be symmetrical, 4 of the same length may be broken at the same time.

Glue and staple them to the forms in progressively shorter lengths. Make sure they are long enough to extend beyond the stem form 2" or more, and also beyond the sheer line.

Trim the Stem

Trim off all the overhanging ends of the strips at each stem form. A fine-tooth **backsaw** is ideal. Hold the saw upside down, cutting upwards from the bottom. Cut right next to the stem form without messing up its masking tape protection. Hold a thin piece of cardboard or wood between the saw teeth and the masking tape. Aim the saw at the edge of the form directly behind it so that it will be parallel to the strips that will be applied later. Cut an angled face on the strips of the first stripped side. This allows the strips on the second side to run out beyond the stem and yet be securely

glued to the strips of the first side.

Check your cut constantly for accuracy by laying a strip alongside the jig in its approximate position. It only needs to be 6' long or so. Follow the curve of the boat around the turn of the bilge by changing the angle of the saw to be parallel to the side of the boat as it curves.

The last two or three strips next to the edge of the football cannot be trimmed by continuing upwards. Use the saw or a knife to make a vertical cut across these strips, in line with the keel strip, down the center of the stem form.

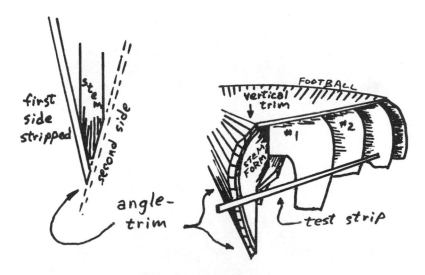

Trimming the overhang

Strip the Second Side

Begin stripping the second side of the boat. The first two or three strips must be stapled into position at all forms except the last two near the stems and then trimmed with a vertical cut to meet the strips of the first side. Use a broken scrap of strip as a straight-edge to mark the cut before trimming with a knife. Finish the trim accurately with a block plane or surform tool. Apply glue to the joint between the strips where they meet on the stem form before stapling down tightly.

After these strips are fitted, glued, and stapled, the rest of the strips for the second side can overhang the stems and must be glued to the strips of the first side where they meet just beyond the stem. Any mistrimmed ends which are too short to meet the strips of the second side will cause gaps. The gaps can be filled in with slivers and chunks of wood whittled to fit. It is better to leave this step until the entire stripping is finished.

You can now see the shape of the boat and its smooth, curving lines. Try to imagine it in motion. The glue-drips and staples block the visual sweep from end to end right now, but there will be a dramatic change when the staples are pulled and the wood is sanded clean, leaving only the longitudinal glue-lines.

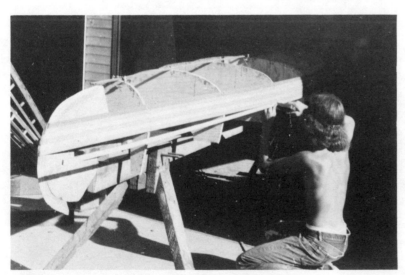

The alternate method; stripping the sides first, starting at approximately the waterline.

Before leaving the boat to cure overnight, double-check all the glue-lines for gaps and rub thickened glue into them with your fingers. Either look up at the light from underneath the boat or put a light on the floor and look down. The light will help you see gaps.

An Alternate Method

The stripping procedure described above is the more efficient of the two methods I have used. The bottom, or football shape, is stripped before the sides in this technique. In the other method, described on page 65 the sides are stripped first. beginning at the waterline for canoes and beginning at the sheer line for kayaks. The football is stripped last, with each piece individually trimmed and fitted carefully into place using a knife and block plane. For kayaks the advantage of this method is that the sheer line can be made absolutely flat, which is of great help when fitting the deck to the hull. So I have included a description of this method in the special section on kayaks.

To use this alternate stripping method on a canoe, arbitrarily select a point near the extreme turn of the bilge, at its sharpest curvature, and staple the first strip there. Make sure that it is level, flat and straight the full length of the boat. This strip will be about four or five strip-widths outside of the football area. From the first strip, strip downwards to complete the entire side of the canoe. Then return to that first strip and work upwards until the stem form is nearly covered, as in making a kayak. That defines the shape of the football, which you then proceed to fill in one strip at a time.

The advantages of this method are that there is no guess work about the shape of the football and the side strips come out nice and straight.

It is possible to splice strips when absolutely necessary. Set up a jig for a saw or sanding wheel so that the scarf is always at the same angle and absolutely flat, or the glue won't hold under the stress of bending around the forms. Make the scarf on the broad face of the strip, glue and clamp overnight.

Sand the Wood

Pull all staples. Hold the wood in, especially near the stem and sheer lines. The staple tends to pull the wood away from the forms, breaking glue joints.

If any of the joints do come apart, use **airplane cement** (Duco) and staples to rejoin them. The staples can be pulled again in about a half-hour. Do not put the boat in hot sun or expansion of the wood will break the glue joints.

Cut the overhanging strips at the stem with a **coping saw** at right angles to the keel line. This will leave a 1/4"-wide blunt edge for the fiberglass to wrap around easily. It will not wrap around a knife edge.

Sanders

Sanding is about half the work of building a boat by this method. It would definitely save a lot of labor to use a power tool. A **disc sander** is the most versatile and fastest tool, but for some people they are too fast and powerful and demand too much skill or too much muscle. A 7" diameter disc sander weighs about 14 lbs. and puts out 1 hp, requiring a light, quick touch. A 5" disc sander is more manageable but slower.

A **belt sander** is relatively easy to control, but it is limited to the exterior of the boat. An **orbital sander** is pretty much limited to finish sanding only and the same is true for hand sanding with a block. Don't use an electric drill with a dimestore disc sanding attachment. Drills are not designed for a long, continuous load, and they will burn out quickly.

Sanding is done with at least two stages: the heavy removal of about 80 to 90 percent of the raised edges and glue, followed by finish sanding. Whatever the technique used, it is very important to feel the boat **through** the sander, as if it were an extension of your hand, and to watch the wood very carefully. Use bright light, keep brushing or blowing the dust away, and pay attention to the scratches or cuts the tool is making. A power tool requires as much or more skill and energy from you as a hand tool. It merely saves time.

Fill all cracks with **plastic wood** after the first stage of sanding. Cracks in the bottom of of the boat will drip resin through during fiberglassing. If you don't like the looks of the staple holes, you can fill them too, but it's a lot of work.

Coarse Sanding

If you assembled the wood with white glue, use a block plane for the first stage of smoothing the boat. Use lengthwise strokes. Then use hand or orbital sanding with 50-grit paper, followed by 80-grit on spruce and other light woods, or 100-grit on cedar, redwood, and other dark woods. Hand sanding should be done with a sanding block. Move the block at a 45° angle across the strips in the bilge area in order to fair the curve, then finish with the grain of the wood.

If you are using a belt sander, sand with the grain and keep the sander flat so it doesn't dig in with an edge of the belt. Move the sander forwards and backwards while working it sideways, making an elongated zig-zag across the boat. In the bilge area, where only the center of the belt is touching the boat, move the sander straight up and down. Use 50-grit paper, and finish with 80- or 100-grit paper.

Use a hard plastic back-up plate behind the sanding discs, and use resin-backed **sanding discs**. Paper-backed floor sanding discs are too fragile for the 7" disc sander powerhouse. Because the 7" is so fast, I recommend that you use 80-grit to start with, unless you find that you can sand without any chop marks and would like to go faster with 60-grit. Chop marks are caused by not holding the disc at a near-flat angle to the wood. When the disc is tipped up, the pressure on its edge causes it to flap and flutter, cutting curved gouges where the flaps hit the wood.

Snug coveralls will help keep you clean and prevent loose shirt-tails from getting tangled up with a 3400 rpm monster. I use a **hat, earplugs, goggles**, and a **dust respirator**, too. Of course, hand sanding is a lot more genteel.

Disc Sander Technique

To use the disc sander, begin on the bottom using a back-and-forth scrubbing motion. Always raise the edge of the disc slightly in the direction of movement so that it doesn't catch an edge and dig in. Make the direction-change quickly at the end of your strokes so that the sander never stops moving while it is in contact with the wood. Do not over-sand an area. Cover a rectangular area with regular strokes, somewhat in rows, until the entire area is almost free of glue and raised edges. Then hit the few remaining spots with short, quick strokes. Stop sanding an area immediately upon reaching a level or smooth condition, or you will be making the hull unnecessarily thin. When first learning how to use the disc sander, turn it off frequently to inspect the results.

On the flat part of the boat's sides, also use a back-and-forth scrubbing motion. I usually kneel on the floor. The sander is close to my face, so I can see what is going on, but I need goggles to keep my eyes free of dust. Leaning over the side to work is worse—it hurts my back. If you sit or crouch to do this part, be super careful not to accidentally bring the edge of the disc across the top of your leg. It cuts.

On the turn of the bilge, use strokes in one direction only (until you get the hang of it), downward at a 45° angle. The disc sander must be rotated from near-horizontal at the edge of the football to vertical on the side.

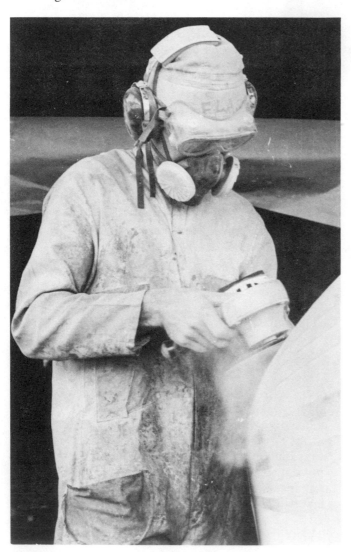

Rolling the disc sander down the turn of the bilge

For right-handers, use the right wrist and elbow with a rolling motion to provide the pivoting momentum. Cradle it somewhat like a baby so it pivots easily in the left hand. Try to use the upper left quadrant of the disc as the part that remains in flat contact with the boat and does the sanding.

It is better to make many light strokes than to try to remove a lot of material at once. Heavy strokes create a dish-shaped path behind them, leaving concave scallops in the boat.

Finish Sanding

The finish sanding can be done with a disc sander if you can obtain a stiff sponge rubber pad called a **feathering disc** from an auto-body tool supplier. The salesman can tell you how to use the **contact cement** to adhere the paper sanding discs to its surface. A 100-grit paper would be best, but 80-grit or 120-grit is acceptable. Use the same motions and techniques as for disc sanding with the hard resin discs. Be careful not to snag one of the broken edges of the strips along the sheer line.

When the finish sanding is done with an orbital sander, scrub the boat lengthwise, with the grain of the wood, in an oval motion. Use 80-grit on light color woods, 100-grit on darker woods.

As a finishing touch, wrap some 50- or 80-grit around a small block of wood and round the stem to a blunt semi-circle. Dust off the entire boat. This is a very sensual point in the construction of a strip boat, for its surface is clean and baby-skin smooth, glowing softly in the light, and the odor of the wood is everywhere.

Lao Tse says, "Be like water that takes on the shape of the container that holds it." Water is very adaptable; it adapts. We're ninety-eight percent water. We are water. A writer said that a scientist studied water to come to the conclusion that we are water expressing itself. Beautiful. Do you like it? Beautiful, isn't it? So you must adapt yourself to reality, like clouds.

ALEXANDRO JODOROWSKY

Fiberglass the Outside

Primer Coat

A primer coat of **lacquer sanding sealer** or a clear brushing lacquer will improve adhesion and prevent resin from soaking into the wood, which increases the weight of the boat. It is recommended for all woods, but is only necessary for cedar and redwood. This method of bonding resin to cedar and redwood is not 100% foolproof, but from my experience with a variety of primer methods, put together with the advice of a PhD organic-polyester chemist, it seems to be a practical method. For cedar and redwood, apply 3 coats of lacquer with a half-hour drying time between coats. For other, non-oily woods, one generous coat should be enough.

As an alternative, second-choice method, I have had fairly good success with a primer coat of resin thinned with no more than 10% styrene monomer and catalyzed with 2% to 4% catalyst, depending on the temperatures. In other words, it has to be mixed "hot" to compensate for the thinness of the film applied to the wood. It may also be true that the extra catalyst tends to overwhelm any of the cure-inhibiting lignins in the wood, thereby insuring a good bond to the cloth layer which follows. Be sure that this coat has no wax, or surfacing agent, in it, and cures to a firm, tacky surface. The resin should be thinned to the viscosity of ordinary varnish. Read ahead to the section on catalyzation.

Lightly sand the dry lacquer by hand, simply to knock down the dust-burrs and rough the surface slightly. Dust off.

Set aside about 6 hours of time to do the fiberglassing. It is possible to interrupt the process if necessary, but the best adhesion between coats is achieved by doing the whole process in one block of time. Prepare adequate ventilation and heat. The styrene monomer vapors may produce headache and nausea. If you are going to do more than one boat, or a kayak, I recommend that you obtain a respirator mask with a filter for organic vapors, or damage to sinuses and lungs may result.

Lay Out the Cloth

Unroll a layer of **cloth** over the boat, from end to end. If it is 60" wide, fold it in half, and cut it to 30" wide. This is the half-layer for covering an area just a little bit larger than the football. 30" cloth usually reaches to the third strip away from the football's edge. A short tongue of cloth may extend out onto the stem, but trim it off where it naturally wants to fold and separate from the wood.

Unroll another layer of cloth over the boat, full width. Be careful not to disturb the half-layer underneath. It helps a lot to have a friend at the other end, holding the cloth stretched out like a tent over the boat. Slowly lower the cloth onto the boat. Check to be sure it reaches all the way to the sheer line on both sides.

The purpose of the next two steps is to get the cloth down tight. Stand at the stem, grab the cloth at top center, and gently tug it tight along the keel line. With two hands just to the right and left of this point, gently tug again, and then move the hands a little further, repeatedly pulling the cloth lengthwise, working

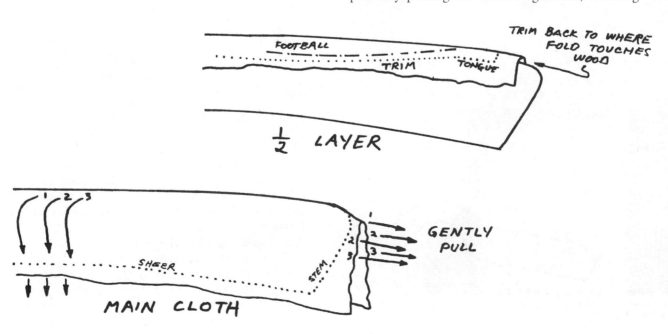

down to the bottom corners of the cloth. A partner may simultaneously oppose your tugs from the opposite end of the boat, or you can pull on each end in two steps. At the end of this step, the longitudinal slack should be pulled out of the cloth, leaving only horizontal slack.

Stand beside the boat at the center, grasp the edge of the cloth with the heel of the hand, and gently tug the wrinkles or slack out. Walk toward the end of the boat, repeatedly giving gentle tugs to the edge of the cloth. Do this for the other 3 quarters of the boat.

Trim the edge of the cloth with **scissors**. Glass fibres are very abrasive, so be prepared to re-sharpen the scissors. Trim two inches below the sheer line and about 1/4" behind the stem. Separate strips will be cut to cover the stem. Trim as high on the stem as necessary to eliminate the fold. The cloth should lie down smooth on the top of the stem.

From scraps of cloth cut strips 4" wide by as long as you can make them, at a 45° angle across the threads of the cloth (bias cut). Cut enough cloth to cover the stem completely two times and to reinforce the top of the stem with 3 to 4 layers. Lay them out nice and neat in two piles, one near each end, so they are ready to grab.

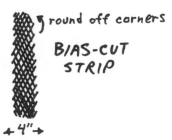

round off corners

BIAS-CUT STRIP

← 4" →

Prepare brushes, **rollers**, **roller pans**, **resin**, **catalyst**, **measuring** and **mixing containers**. The roller pan must be new and chromed since polyester will dissolve any paint and transfer it to the boat. Rollers are far more efficient than brushes for this work.

Lay old **newspapers** on the floor under the edge of the boat, unless you don't care about the floor. Buy or make a roller **squeegee** out

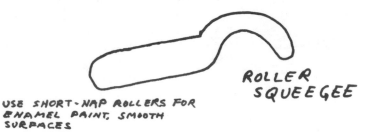

ROLLER SQUEEGEE

USE SHORT-NAP ROLLERS FOR ENAMEL PAINT, SMOOTH SURFACES

of a thin wood scrap. Set up a cleanup area on old newspapers, with **acetone** and a spare roller tray ready. **Ammonia** and **hot water** may be used for cleanup if you are careful to dry everything before it comes in contact with resin.

Test the Resin

Pour 4 ounces of your resin into a dixie cup and if it is pure resin without promoter, add .5% of cobalt **promoter** or .25% of cobalt-DMA promoter. Do not allow promoter and catalyst to come into direct contact with each other full strength. A fire or explosion may result. Use the chart in the appendix to decide on the rate of catalyzation. It may be torn out and posted on your wall.

A **veterinary syringe** is a safe and accurate tool for measuring catalyst. Pour a few ounces of catalyst into a **glass** or **polyethylene** or **waxed paper cup**, and then suck the correct amount into the syringe. Slowly press the plunger and allow the catalyst to fall into the resin. A hard squirt may splash catalyst into your eyes. If you should ever get any catalyst on your hands, eyes, nose, mouth, etc., flush immediately with plenty of water. Neutralize it with lemon juice or vinegar.

Stir the catalyst into the 4 oz. of resin, and then time the interval to its gelation. It should be a minimum of 20 minutes and a maximum of 30 minutes. The gel time in the pot is faster than the gel time on the boat, because the heat builds up faster in a mass than in a film. A gel time of 20 minutes in the pot usually means a gel time of 30 minutes on the boat for the same resin-promoter-catalyst combination. Modify your catalysation rate until you achieve a proper gel time.

Apply the Resin

At least 2½ quarts of **resin** is needed to saturate 1½ layers of 6 oz. cloth on a 17' Micmac. If this is your first experience at fiberglassing, you will probably use 3 quarts. Bear in mind that the chemical reaction which causes the gelation and cure of the resin will speed up with higher temperatures and slow down with lower temperatures. The temperature of the resin is affected by where it is stored, the temperature of the cloth and the wood, and, least of all, it is affected by the temperature of the air in the room at the moment of its application.

It will be difficult to work with the resin if it is too thick, which it sometimes is, but not usually. Resin viscosity should be like heavy pancake syrup, or hot honey. It should not be as slow to pour as cold honey, or even room temperature honey. If you need to thin the resin use styrene monomer. Do not use more than 10%, i.e., more than 3 ounces of styrene per quart of resin.

The resin is applied in several small batches so that you have plenty of time to use it up before it gels. Into a clean container pour 20 to 30 ounces of resin. No surfacing wax is needed until the final covering coat of resin. If your resin has surfacing wax already in it, the covering coats must be applied within 20 minutes of the gel time of the previous coat of resin. Catalyze your first batch of resin, and stir it thoroughly.

Begin applying the resin in the center of the bottom. Pour a puddle of resin directly onto the boat. Spread the resin out with the roller until the cloth has soaked up the resin, leaving no puddle or glossy spot. The cloth should be completely transparent when it is saturated, and down tight on the wood. Too much resin will float the glass off the wood and make a heavy, weak laminate. Too little resin leaves air bubbles and white-opaque starved spots. The cloth should look uniformly silky-wet.

Rolling

Roll back and forth several times in one area to work the resin into the glass fibres and help the air bubbles to the surface. Do not roll with so much pressure that the cloth bunches up into wrinkles or starts to move around. Roll in a direction diagonal to the weave of the cloth.

The wetted area should be the shape of a diamond, approximately, so that as it spreads towards the stems the keel line is wetted before the sheer line. This helps wrinkles to move towards the edges of the cloth. Always keep a well-defined edge to the saturated area, and do not allow drips to fall onto the dry areas. If the saturated area gels before new resin is added to its border, there may be permanent wrinkles in the cloth along its edge unless that edge is kept neat.

Cloth takes time to absorb resin, and it cannot be rushed. The best strategy is quickly to spread out most of the resin, and then go back over it several times with the roller. Flooding an area will speed up the absorption in the double layer across the football, but the excess resin must be carried away by the roller to dry areas. Do not squeegee a puddle of resin in front of the roller down the side of the boat, or it will land on the floor and be wasted. Pick up a moderate amount of resin on the roller from the bottom of the boat, and then roll it onto the side of the boat.

Mix a second batch of resin after the first is gone. It is not necessary to clean the rollers or to use a different container for mixing unless it is getting close to gel time. If the resin gels in the roller or bucket, it will make lumps in the next batch.

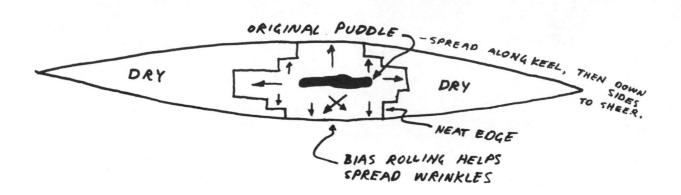

ORIGINAL PUDDLE — SPREAD ALONG KEEL, THEN DOWN SIDES TO SHEER.

DRY

DRY

NEAT EDGE

BIAS ROLLING HELPS SPREAD WRINKLES

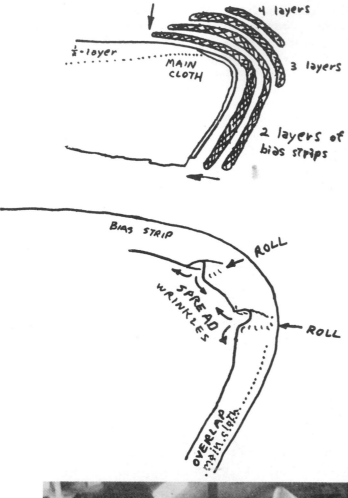

*Use metal or paper buckets to mix resin—
polyethylene will melt when the resin gets hot!*

Stem Strips

After the entire main cloth is wetted out, lay the bias-cut strips over the stems. Wet each layer separately. Wrinkles will often come out very easily if you roll very gently on these strips from the edge of the stem towards the edge of the strip.

When all is done, scrape the excess resin from the roller and clean it in **acetone**. Roll the roller in acetone, then squeegee the acetone from the roller and roll it out on newspapers a few times.

If there are any air bubbles larger than a nickel under the cloth, inject catalyzed resin into them with a veterinary syringe and a **no. 18 needle**. On the side of the boat, inject the bubble from the top side so gravity will hold the resin in. If the fiberglass bends your needle because it is too hard already, drill a tiny hole.

Covering Coats

Allow the resin to gel to a tacky surface. For a 17' Micmac, catalyze 50 ounces of resin for the first covering coat. Pour the resin into a roller pan and roll a heavy coat of resin onto the boat. Roll upwards from the sheer to the keel so that it doesn't run off onto the floor. Roll about two roller-widths, distributing the coat evenly, and re-wet the roller. It should take less than ten minutes to coat the boat entirely. Clean up.

Allow the first covering coat to gel. The first coat is the heaviest, since the weave of the cloth gives it something to hang onto. The second and third coats should be smaller quantities. How many coats and what quantity of resin in each is a matter for individual judgment. My rule of thumb is to apply one more coat after the cloth texture disappears. Thick resin may do it in two coats, thin resin may need four. If your resin does not have **surfacing wax** already in it, stir one ounce per quart into the final coat of resin, and be very careful to get complete coverage with the last coat. Any spots not covered with wax will remain glossy after gel time and can be covered with a **paste car wax**.

Allow the boat to cure overnight.

Sand the Resin and the Wood Inside

Sanding the covering coats of resin will give the boat a smooth surface for slipping and sliding through the water. It can be done with the same tools and techniques used for sanding the exterior of the wood. However, begin with a much lighter, finer grit of sandpaper. Although the resin will not sand as fast as the wood, you should take great care not to sand into the cloth, cutting the fibres that hold the boat together.

For the first stage of sanding, I recommend 80- or 100-grit for power sanding with disc or belt, and 60-grit for orbital sanders. For all sanding jobs, and particularly on resin, it pays to buy **aluminum oxide paper** instead of garnet or flint. To prevent clogging on resin, use open coat papers, or the dry lubricant type.

For the finish stage of sanding, use 120-grit on the feathering disc or 100-grit on the orbital sander. This prepares the surface for varnishing, the final completing step, much later.

Use a dust respirator while disc or belt sanding. If any glass particles are inhaled, they accumulate in your lungs as a permanent feature. The cloth strips wrapped around the stems are the one place where you deliberately sand into the cloth fibres, in order to feather the edges of those strips into the main body of the boat.

Instead of varnish, the hull may be finished to a gloss finish by wet sanding by hand, in steps from 180-grit to 220, 320, 400, 600, rubbing compound, and wax. Another alternative gloss finish is clear gloss epoxy enamel. Personally, I feel gloss finish is fine for racing, but for aesthetics I prefer a satin finish.

Mark the sheer line. Use a long strip clamped in place alongside the edge of the boat, as an edge to draw against. Clamp the strip at the middle of the side with two clamps, one on each side of the center form, about a foot or so apart, to hold it level there. Clamp it again at the tip of the stem, bending the strip into a long natural curve. Scratch or draw a line on the resin.

Remove Boat from Forms

Prepare a **cradle** to accept the boat right side up. Large cardboard cartons with a shallow curve cut into their top edges are cheap and fast. You could use saw-horses, tables, chairs, or scrap lumber to make one to order. Make the cradle high enough so that you don't ruin your back while working on the inside of the boat.

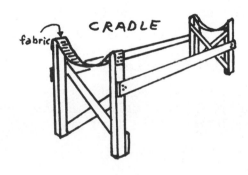

CRADLE
fabric

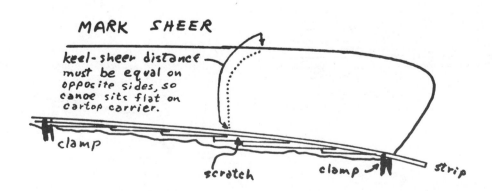

MARK SHEER

keel-sheer distance
must be equal on
opposite sides, so
canoe sits flat on
cartop carrier.

clamp

scratch   clamp   strip

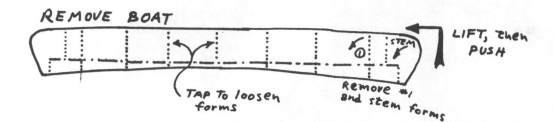

REMOVE BOAT

TAP To loosen forms

Remove #1 and stem forms

LIFT, then PUSH

STEM

Remove the boat from the forms. At one end of the strongback, remove the stem form and the first form behind it. A sharp tap with a hammer on those forms and all the others should be enough to loosen them. Grasp the boat at the end where the stem form is removed, lift vertically, and push towards the other end.

When the boat is loose and propped up on the forms, two people should carefully lift and roll the boat over and transfer it to the cradle. Be aware that the boat, especially if it is a long one, may fold in half when it is supported only by the stems in the keel-down position. Either give it some support in the middle or keep it upside down until it is in the cradle.

Did you feel surprised to see the inside of the boat? A boat keel-down is a completely different feeling from a boat keel-up.

The jig can be used over again for making several boats. Sooner or later somebody may ask you for it, so save it if you can.

pressure QUICKLY

Trim the Sheer

Trim the sheer-line with coping saw or sabre saw. Use a **fiberglass-cutting blade** or **hacksaw** blade. Hold the boat's edge firmly. If possible, aim the teeth of the blade so that they pull the fiberglass towards, not away, from the wood. The trimmed-off piece should be cut into short sections as you go along, so that a long piece of it doesn't fall to the floor and pull fiberglass off the wood with its weight.

Sand the Inside

Use a **wood rasp** to clean off the glue and resin drips, raised edges on the interior of the boat, including the apex of the boat. Sweep the boat clean of debris.

If you have a disc sander, prepare it for sanding the inside. Use a soft rubber **buffing back-up plate** behind an 80-grit sanding disc. Black & Decker makes one called a super-flexible, which I use. Remove the side-handles. Don your goggles, respirator, ear plugs, hat, and coveralls.

The football area and the sides are relatively flat. Use a straight, back-and-forth motion similar to that used on the exterior. Use a light touch near the sheer line in order to preserve the thickness of the wood.

Use a different technique for the bilge area. Grasp the sander by its trigger handle and its nose. Brace your stomach and hips against the side of the canoe so that it doesn't slide around. Lean over the side of the canoe so that your head almost touches the bottom of the canoe. Press the sanding disc into the bilge of the canoe without turning it on—this is a dry run. Press the edge of the disc with enough force to flatten it against the wood, while the remainder of the disc does not touch the wood. I prefer to flatten the disc edge which is "downhill" from the sander, so the weight of the sander helps to do the pushing. Now practice a little of the motion, making short, quick oval strokes up and down in the bilge, clockwise ovals when holding the sander to

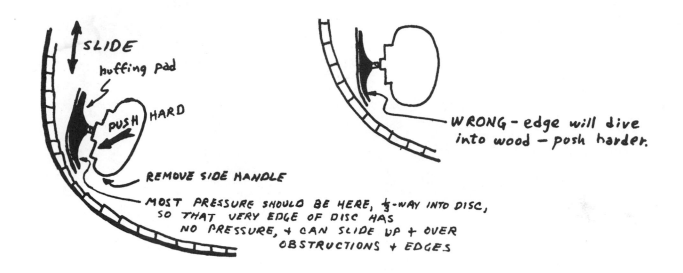

SLIDE

buffing pad

PUSH HARD

REMOVE SIDE HANDLE

MOST PRESSURE SHOULD BE HERE, $\frac{1}{3}$-WAY INTO DISC,
SO THAT VERY EDGE OF DISC HAS
NO PRESSURE, + CAN SLIDE UP + OVER
OBSTRUCTIONS + EDGES

WRONG - edge will dive
into wood - posh harder.

the right, counter-clockwise ovals to the left. The oval pattern insures that any raised edges will be smoothed down with the trailing edge of the disc. If the leading edge catches a raised edge of wood, it will dive into the wood, making a gouge.

Lift the sander off the wood, turn it on, and touch down in the middle of the bilge, moving in the oval pattern as you touch. Use plenty of force to deform the disc flat against the wood. When you are ready to take a break, lift off smoothly, in motion, before stopping. The sander will get hot and can be cooled off by allowing it to run freely. This technique can be used across the bottom in the areas of tight curvature near the stems. You will not be able to sand completely into the ends of the boat. Avoid the groove at the base of the

stem, because the edge of the disc will catch and dive.

Finish Sanding

Finish sanding is used to eliminate the last of the glue and raised edges and the scratches of the disc sander. Scratches will not be easily visible through the textured fiberglass on the inside, compared to the clear finish on the outside. 60-grit paper is suitable. An excellent sander for this job is the Rockwell 330A Speed-bloc, with a sponge rubber pad cut into a curve to fit the bilge.

Other techniques for sanding the inside of the boat may be used, but the disc sander is the only one I am familiar with.

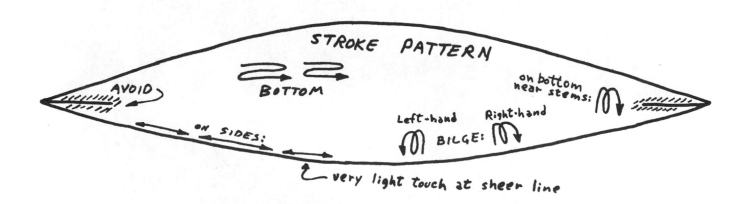

STROKE PATTERN

AVOID

BOTTOM

on SIDES:

on bottom near stems:

Left-hand   Right-hand

BILGE:

very light touch at sheer line

The highest motive is to be like water.
Water is essential to all living things,
*   yet it demands no pay or recognition.*
Rather it flows humbly to the lowest level.
Nothing is weaker than water, yet for
*   overcoming what is hard and strong,*
*   nothing surpasses it.*

LAO TSE

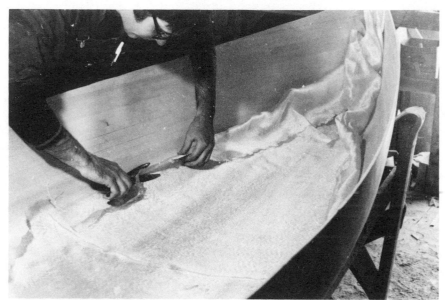

Trimming the half-layer

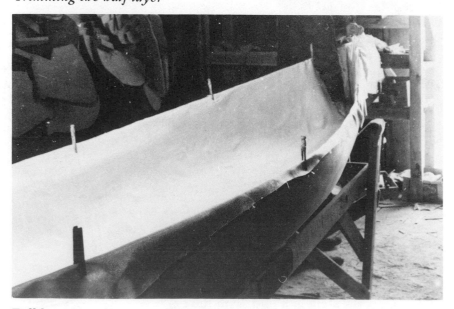

Full layer installed

Fiberglass the Inside

Clean all the dust out from the inside with **brush, vacuum,** or **blower.** Save some for the next step.

Fill the Stem

Catalyze 12 oz. of resin (for canoe) at the rate of 4%. Slowly add **sanding dust** while stirring until you have a gelatinous paste. A glob of it should settle and flow very slowly when put on a flat surface.

Dip a **1" wide brush** into acetone, and lightly shake off the brush. The acetone helps the paste slip off the brush, and, in small amounts, it doesn't hurt the resin cure. Use the brush as a spatula to spread the paste into the apex of the boat, the stem. Try not to be sloppy. The paste that falls onto the sides or bottom of the boat can be cleaned up with a brush lightly coated with acetone, but it would be better if the job were done neatly the first time. Form a U-shape with the paste in the V of the stem, stroking and molding it with the acetone-coated brush.

Primer Coat

Apply a **lacquer sealer** coat to the interior of the boat, one coat for spruce, three coats for cedar or redwood. Allow to dry.

Sand the lacquer lightly, and dust out the boat.

Lay Out the Cloth

Cover the bottom of the boat with a half-layer of cloth, 30" wide for canoes. Gently pull the slack out of the cloth, and sweep the wrinkles towards the edges, across the bias of the cloth. In the ends of the boat, the excess cloth can be folded in towards the middle. Trim the cloth from 2" to 4" outside the edge of the football. Allow a tongue to extend into the stem.

Suspend the main cloth piece over the boat, then allow it to sag into the boat. Sweep the cloth wrinkles and slack out of the bottom of the boat, and tack the cloth to the sheer line with **clothespins.** Leave a small amount of slack, bagginess, in the sides.

In order to get the main cloth right up to the stem, slide your hand into the folds of cloth at the end of the boat, and coax the folds past your fingertips so that it lays smoothly against the side of the boat. The main cloth should meet the stem in a fold, with the excess material in the middle.

Trim along the apex of this fold with scissors, beginning at the top and going down as far as you can reach, or until you become tangled in more bunched-up folds. Then cut horizontally across the excess material, meeting your vertical cut and removing all that material that was obscuring your vision. After you have cut vertically into the very extreme apex of the canoe, cut horizontally from the base of the stem. Begin the horizontal cut where the main cloth starts to wrinkle up. Continue trimming away the excess until, like the exterior main cloth, the cloth comes to within about 1" of the stem of the boat.

Trim the cloth that hangs over the sheer line, about 3" outside the sheer. From the scraps of cloth cut some bias strips similar to those used on the outside of the stem, only not so many. Only one layer of strips is necessary to cover the interior of the stem.

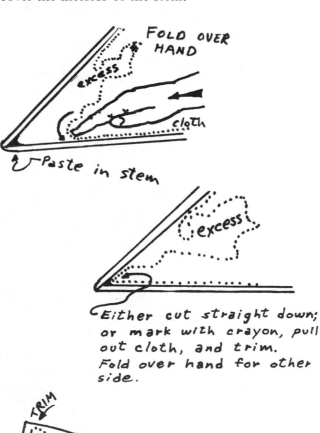

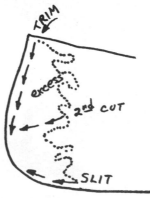

Apply Resin

The cloth layup on the inside is usually identical to the exterior, with the exception that there are no covering coats of resin to smooth out the texture of the cloth. Therefore, **surfacing wax** must be in the first (and only) coat of resin.

Make ready a clean roller, natural bristle brush and a mixing container. A roller pan is not needed. Prepare the first batch with surfacing agent and catalyst, mixed in separately. I suggest you work with smaller batches than used on the exterior, since the probability of difficulties is greater, requiring more time. Twenty ounces might be a good start.

Pour the resin into the bottom of the canoe in a long puddle. Roll the resin gently outwards towards the sides and ends. Roll slowly at first so that the cloth sticks to the boat instead of the roller, which has a tendency to pick it up. If rolling the cloth into the bilge area on one side of the boat pulls cloth out of the opposite bilge, untack the edge of the cloth at the sheer line, and give the cloth more slack. Remove the clothespins as you come to them.

Wrinkles may occur in the half-layer of cloth underneath the main layer. If your attempts to roll out the wrinkles fail you will have to reach under the main cloth with your hand in order to pull out the slack.

Watch out for drips of resin running down the outside of the boat, caused by rolling too much resin up to the sheer. Check the sheer for wrinkles in the cloth—move them towards the ends of the boat. Put on enough resin to saturate the cloth, making it transparent and silk-textured, but not enough to cause runs and puddles.

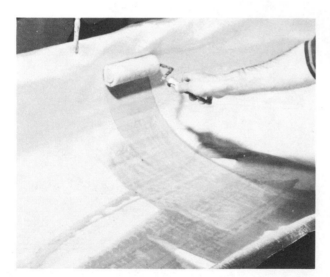

Rolling resin from the puddle up the side

Gently pulling out a wrinkle

In the ends of the boat, use small batches with slightly less catalyst, and a **3" wide brush**. Use the brush to squeegee the resin toward the stem. After the main cloth is wetted completely into the end, fold a bias-cut strip over the bristles of the brush. Carry the strip into the apex, holding its loose end up with the other hand. Squeeze the strip against the stem for a moment, then slowly press the rest of the strip into place with the brush and saturate the strip.

The cloth overhanging the sheer may be trimmed about 45 minutes after gel time, or the next day, with a **utility knife**. Because the styrene gases sink into the boat and in-hibit the cure, you may need to fan them out of the boat. Allow the resin to cure overnight.

Prepare Air Chamber Panels

Prepare panels of strips and glass for cutting out the teardrop shape of the air chamber bulkheads, to be installed later. On a **3' x 4' piece of scrap** anything that will hold a staple leg, lay down a layer of **polyethylene** or two layers of **wax paper** so that the resin won't stick to it.

Prepare 14 strips left over from stripping into 3' lengths. If you have no strips, 1/8" to 1/4" plywood may substitute. On top of the plastic or waxed paper, lay down one layer of cloth. Use up your leftovers, and overlap the seams an inch or two. Saturate the cloth with about 8 ounces of catalyzed resin.

Press strips into the wet cloth, side by side and staple them to the backing material, making a panel of strips 3' long by 14 strips wide. If you are using plywood for the panel, simply fiberglass one side of the plywood and skip all the waxed paper and backing board.

Allow the panel to cure overnight. Pull all the staples except two near the corners to hold it down. Sand the panel smooth, with coarse-medium grit followed by fine. Pull the re-maining staples. Set aside.

Using the brush near the end

Installing the bias-cut strip

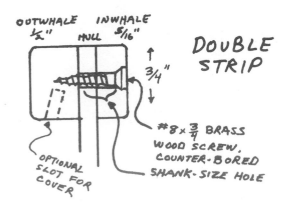

Double-strip design is light weight and simple

More traditional looking and heavier, the spacer-block design is stiffer. Note flat bar seats and thwarts hung on long bolts from spacer block. Also note ash decks.

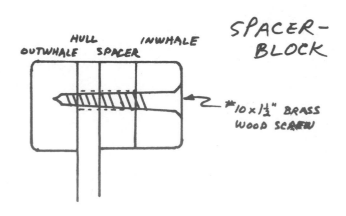

OUTWHALE   INWHALE
½"   HULL   5/16"

DOUBLE
STRIP

↑
¾"
↓

#8 x ¾ BRASS
WOOD SCREW,
COUNTER-BORED
SHANK-SIZE HOLE

OPTIONAL
SLOT FOR
COVER

HULL   INWHALE
OUTWHALE   SPACER

SPACER-
BLOCK

#10 x 1½" BRASS
WOOD SCREW

Finishing Touches

Gunnel Design

Gunnels (gunwales) protect the edge of the boat from wear against docks, cartop carriers, loading and unloading packs. They also stiffen the edge and provide a structural member for the mounting of thwarts, seats or the lashing-in gear. Gunnels vary a lot in design. Two of the simplest and most popular are shown here.

The advantage of the spacer-block design is more lashing points. However, it is complex to install and adds excess weight.

For stiffness and durability choose oak or ash. Oak is 10% heavier than ash but their other physical properties are the same. If you can get it, Honduras mahogany is also suitable. Philippine mahogany tends to shatter and split—avoid it. For lighter weight, sacrificing some durability, you may use spruce, cedar, pine or fir. For hardwoods in the double-strip design gunnel, use 1/2" x 3/4" for the outwale and 5/16" x 3/4" for the inwale. Softwoods should have slightly larger dimensions, and the inwale of the spacer-block design should be larger. Spacer-blocks should be 1/4" x 3/4" x 2" and varnished before installation.

Gunnel Installation

The easiest way to install a spacer-block gunnel is to pre-glue the spacer blocks to the inwale before installation, so that they become part of the inwale. Installation proceeds similar to double-strip design gunnels.

The inside surfaces of the inwale and outwale should be sealed with **varnish** or a **sealer** before installation, to prevent swelling later.

Do not design a gunnel to cover the top edge of the sheer line. Water will get trapped there and begin a delamination of the fiberglass. The top edge of the sheer should be exposed and varnished at the same time the gunnel is varnished.

Temporarily clamp the outwale and inwale in position on the side of the canoe with three or four **clamps**, The gunnel is to be installed approximately ¼" below the edge of the sheer, and the sheer is planed or sanded down to the edge of the gunnel after installation.

Round off one end of the inwale. Adjust its position so that it is 6" from the tip of the stem, assuming that you intend to have a short thwart instead of a solid deck. Otherwise, design the deck and adjust the inwale accordingly.

With the inwale in position, cut it off 6" behind the opposite stem and round it off.

Detail of inwale rounded off; short thwart beveled to meet inwale

Splicing

If it is necessary to splice pieces of wood
together to create a long enough gunnel, overlap the ends of the pieces to be spliced, one
on top of the other, and clamp them securely
at the ends of the overlap. Then saw vertically through both pieces to create a long, tapering scarf joint. This joint can be glued prior
to, or during, assembly on the boat. I usually
do it on the boat, and locate the joint at a
place where there are screws to reinforce it.

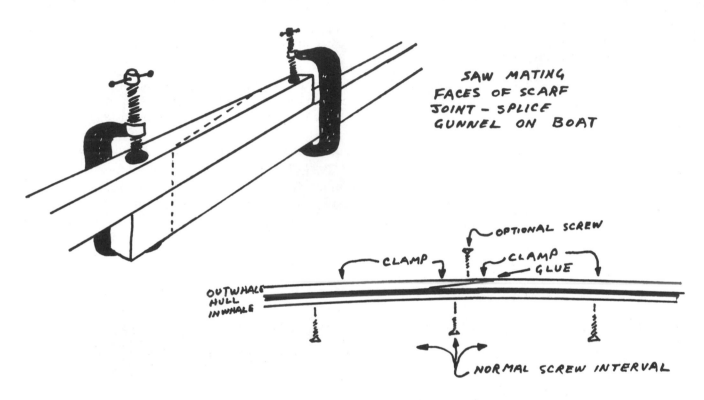

SAW MATING
FACES OF SCARF
JOINT - SPLICE
GUNNEL ON BOAT

OPTIONAL SCREW

CLAMP   CLAMP
GLUE

OUTWHALE
HULL
INWHALE

NORMAL SCREW INTERVAL

Mark Screw Positions

Use a **tape measure** to find the mid-point
of the sheer line, the balance point of the
boat. Stretch the tape from the tip of
one stem to a point near the center of the
sheer and mark the nearest whole foot
(usually 8') on the sheer. Repeat from
the other end of the boat and then measure
the distance between the two marks and
divide.

Unless you want a single thwart at the
mid point find the portage thwarts'
positions by measuring 7½" to either
side of the mid point of the sheer.

Measure and mark the position of the short
thwart, 12" from the tip of the stem.
Canoes 18' and longer should have additional
thwarts: one behind the bow seat, and one
sufficiently forward of the stern seat to
give the paddler some leg room. These
additional thwarts are necessary because when
a canoe is tossing up and down in waves
the forces on the hull tend to push the sides
apart. The thwarts hold the sides of the boat
together. The fastenings of seat bars
are not adequate to do this.

Between the short thwart and the portage or
center thwarts, mark the positions for screws.
Usually a distance of 8¼" will divide the space
fairly evenly. Spacer-block gunnels might
need screws only 6" apart. Also mark positions for screws at the mid-point between the
portage thwarts, at the end of the inwale (far
enough back to prevent splitting) and at the
end of the outwale.

Clamp

Approximately between every alternate screw position clamp the inwale and outwale to the side of the boat with the C-clamps, padding their jaws with wood scraps. You probably don't have enough clamps to do the entire side of the boat at once, so simply begin at one end and work towards the other end of the canoe. Leap-frog the clamps onward after drilling and screwing. Adjust the inwale and outwale into their final positions, being careful that one is not lower than the other on the side of the boat. Leave the edge of the sheer projecting above the gunnel slightly. Put the handles of the C-clamps projecting inwards, so they don't catch you in the gut or snag the drill's power cord.

Select the appropriate size **flat-head brass wood screw**. It should reach through the inwale and hull into the middle of the outwale. A 3/4'' long #8 screw is right for a 5/16'' thick inwale and 1/2'' thick outwale in the double-strip design which I use. A spacer block design may need a screw as long as 1½''. For the 8 screws installed from the outside at the end of the inwale and the end of the outwale, I use a 1'' x #8 screw.

Drill

Use a **drill bit** specially designed for wood screws. Stanley makes one called "Screw-Mate." The counter-bore feature helps to make a neater job. At the tip of the outwale, about 1'' back from the tip, drill through the outwale into the stem. Aim carefully with a backward slanting angle and drill deep enough to bury the head of the screw into the outwale.

At the tip of the inwale drill again from the outside of the canoe, through the hull into the inwale, deep enough so the tip of the screw will hold the inwale.

Do not drill holes at the thwart positions now. The thwart's screws, installed later, will also hold the gunnel together. Drill the rest of the screw holes through the inwale into the outwale. Counter-bore about 1/8''. Insert screws into all the holes and pull the inwale and outwale tightly together against the hull. Sometimes this means that the hole has to be re-drilled slightly oversize through the inwale and hull.

Gunnel strips clamped and marked, ready for drilling

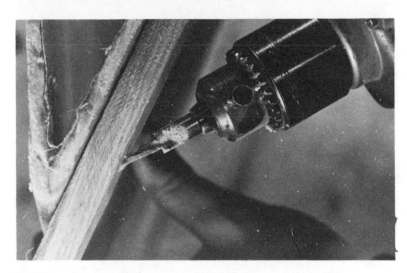

Drilling the top of the outwale with a screw-mate bit.

When you reach the far end of the canoe, again drill screw holes from the outside at the tip of the inwale and at the tip of the outwale. Remove all clamps. Trim any outwale which overhangs beyond the stem. Repeat the entire gunnel installation for the opposite side.

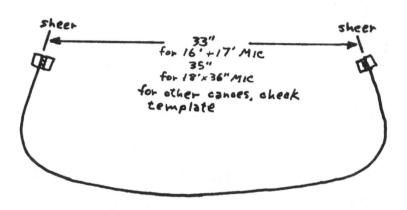

sheer   sheer

33"
for 16' + 17' MIC
35"
for 18' x 36" MIC
for other canoes, check
template

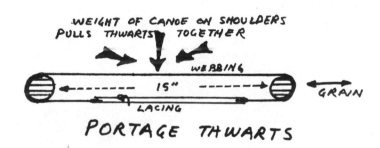

WEIGHT OF CANOE ON SHOULDERS
PULLS THWARTS TOGETHER

WEBBING

15"

LACING   GRAIN

PORTAGE THWARTS

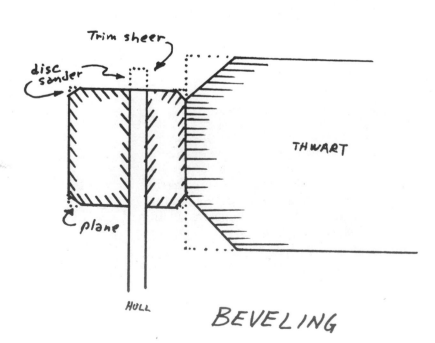

Trim sheer

disc
sander

THWART

plane

HULL   BEVELING

Trim the Sheer

Trim the sheer line down flush to the gunnel with a surform tool or a disc sander. Use the disc sander like a plane, making long, sweeping strokes. Use a medium grit, then a fine grit. A block plane is not recommended because the fiberglass will ruin its edge.

Use the sander, plane, or surform to bevel the corners of the gunnel. The disc sander may be used on the corner while walking from one end of the boat to the other.

Install Thwarts

At the center thwarts, or the portage thwarts, the sheer lines should be 33" apart for the 16' and 17' Micmac, and 35" for the 18' Micmac. Sometimes the boat needs to be spread, sometimes pulled together. In any case, do not try to alter its shape too much, or a sharp bend will occur in the sheer from the excessive push or pull. You may have to use a slightly different length thwart. I use **1¼" fir dowel** (closet rod) because it is rigid and light.

The portage thwarts should have their grain aligned horizontally, so that they are most rigid in the direction of stress. Also, the tumblehome and the taper towards the end of the boat require a slight bevel on their ends so that they fit the inwale tightly. The same is true of thwarts closer to the ends of the boat. A sailing thwart, usually behind the bow seat, should be a 1" x 4" piece of oak or ash or a 2" x 4" of cedar, and bored to accommodate the mast.

The thwart centered on the inwale will protrude above and below, since it is thicker. Bevel the end of the thwart with a rasp, plane, surform, or sanding block, so that it comes together smoothly with the inwale.

With the thwart held in position, carefully aim a drill bit for **2" long #8 wood screws** and drill two holes into the end of each thwart, inserting the screw in one hole before drilling the one next to it. Again, drill a shank-size hole completely through the outwale, hull and inwale, so that the screw pulls everything together.

The **short thwarts** are installed in similar fashion. If you have a **saw with a tilting table**, set the table at the following angles: 16' Micmac, 20°; 17' Micmac, 16°; 18' Micmac and 16' Abenaki, 15°. Then trim the dowel at that angle on both ends so that their trimmed faces are in converging planes. Trial-fit the short thwart in place, rotating it until it fits. Bevel the ends.

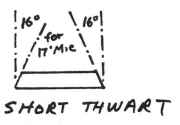

SHORT THWART

Determine Seat Positions

The **seats** in a canoe should be mounted as close to the ends as possible. This provides maximum leverage for steering and a narrow part of the boat to paddle from, minimizing the need to reach out sideways. The limiting factor in this equation is the length of the bow paddler's legs. I usually allow 36" from the front edge of the bow seat to the tip of the football, which will accommodate persons up to 6' in height.

The second consideration is the bow-stern trim of the boat, which should be level. A boat that is down in the bow will oversteer, swinging from side to side in big arcs. A boat that is down in the stern will understeer, which is in most cases desirable for general lake cruising. However, it slows the boat down down—it "mushes" through the water—and inhibits the versatility of the boat for river work. Theoretically, if the same two paddlers are always to sit in the same positions in this canoe you're building, you could tailor the seat positions for that one special situation.

The distance from the stern seat to the center equals the bow seat-to-center distance times the bowman's weight divided by the sternman's weight. In practice, however, other people are likely to use the boat, and sit in other places, using their gear's placement to trim the boat. So I simply place the stern seat's front edge 36" from the tip of the football, the best place for a person of weight equal to that of the bowman.

I mount seats with an 8" clearance under them. This allows me to get my size 12 boot under the seat and back out again, and creates a lower center of gravity. However, for less stability and more efficient use of muscles in paddling, mount the seats with a 10" clearance under them.

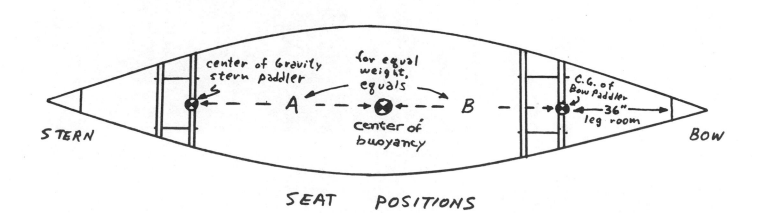

SEAT POSITIONS

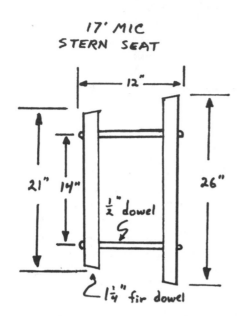

17' MIC
STERN SEAT

12"

21"   14"   26"

½" dowel

1¼" fir dowel

Make Seat Frames

Assemble the seats before installation. If you are mounting them 36" from the tip of the football and 8" off the bottom, the seat bars should be cut to the following lengths:

	Front		Rear	
16' Micmac	30"	27"	23"	27"
17' Micmac	28"	26"	21"	26"
18' Micmac	28"	24"	20"	24"
16' Abenaki	29"	25"	18"	23"

Bevel the ends of all bars 8°.

If using other seat positions, use a broken strip to approximate the leading edge of the seat at the appropriate height. Mark the position of the seat bar on the inside of the canoe and measure the length of the seat bar. Cut the seat bars overlong to allow for trimming as you gradually fit the seat to the boat.

For seat bar stock, I use the same 1¼" **fir dowel** as for the thwarts, since they are so rigid for the weight. The traditional, flat bar of hardwood bends a lot, creating unusual stress at the fastener points.

Cut ½" **hardwood dowel** into 4 pieces, 12" long. Round the ends of each dowel into a blunt point.

Installed dowel seat showing fabric, grommets and lacing

Place each piece of dowel seat bar on the workbench so that the grain is horizontal. Mark the center of its length. Measure 7" from this point in both directions, and mark centers for the ½" holes to be bored next.

The holes **must** be parallel to each other. A **drill press** is very helpful. Drill one of the holes, almost all the way through, and then back-drill it, to prevent splintering. Use a hammer to drive in one of the 1/2" dowels so that its rounded end projects out from the rear side. The front side is the side with the pencil marks.

Clamp the seat bar loosely in position under the drill for the second hole. Sight the drill and the projecting dowel. Adjust the dowel by rotating the seat bar until it is parallel to the drill. Securely clamp and drill and back-drill.

Repeat the above operation for the opposing seat bar, and then drive the two sets of bars together. The front and rear bars of the seat should be parallel.

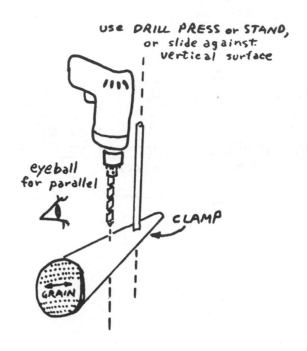

Flat bar seat laced with Dacron rope and bolted to a cleat which is glassed to the hull. The cleat should have a broad surface to bond to the hull and spread out the stress.

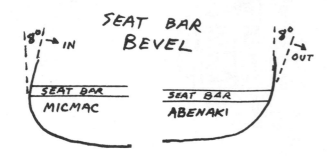

SEAT BAR
BEVEL

8° IN   8°
                                   OUT

SEAT BAR   SEAT BAR
MICMAC   ABENAKI

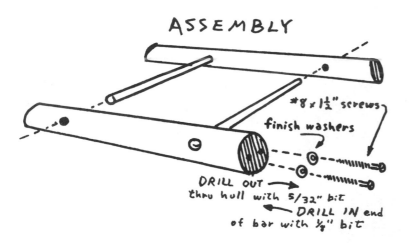

ASSEMBLY

#8 x 1¼" screws
finish washers

DRILL OUT →
thru hull with 5/32" bit
          → DRILL IN end
of bar with ¼" bit

Install Seats

Install the seats in the boat. Lay the seat
across the gunnels as far back from the stem
as possible, still having them supported.
Square it to the keel line of the boat by eye.
Strike a pencil line across their bottom sides,
using the inwales as a pencil guide. Trim along
this line, using a saw with its table set at 8°.
Because of the Micmacs tumblehome, a
seat bar will be slightly shorter end-to-
end across the top than across the bottom.
The Abenaki seat bars have an 8° bevel
in the opposite direction.

Using a **ruler** and a **square**, find the points on
the inside of the canoe that are 36" from the
tip of the football and 8" up from the bottom.
Trial-fit the seat into this position. It should
be a little too large at this point. Continue to
trim small amounts from the ends of the bars
until the fit is full contact on the end of each
bar in the correct position in the boat. A saw
can be used to make the first, larger cuts, and
a rasp and sanding block should be used for
the final touches.

Draw a semicircle around the end of the seat
bar on the interior of the canoe. Drill two
holes outwards, inside the circle, side by side,
using a **bit 5/32" or 3/16" in diameter**. Replace the seat into position, and through the
two holes you just drilled in the hull, drill
inwards into the end of the seat bar with a
bit for 1 **1½" x #8 wood screw**. Insert one
screw, with a **finishing washer** under its head,
before drilling its partner. The finishing
washer is necessary to spread the tensile pull
of the screw head over the surface of the
hull. A drop of varnish in the screw hole before inserting the screw helps to seal the
hole.

Finish-sand the seats, thwarts, and gunnels
with 80- or 100-grit sandpaper. Round all
corners. The 120-grit disc sander scratches in
the ash or oak gunnels will be invisible when
varnished.

Cut Out Bulkheads

Lay out the pattern for the **air chamber bulkhead** on the panels prepared previously. Align the axis of the teardrop with the strips. Cut out with the sabersaw, coping saw, or bandsaw. Again, a hacksaw blade or fiberglass cutting blade will last longer than a wood-cutting blade. Take great care to prevent chattering, or the joints between the strips will break open.

With a coarse sandpaper on a block, bevel the edge of the bulkhead inwards toward the fiberglass side of the piece. Trial fit the bulkhead into the apex of the canoe, bare wood side facing out. The tip of the teardrop should be about 2" below the tip of the stem. Continue sanding off the high spots until the smallest gap is about a pencil-line thick. Use a pencil to mark the high spots. The bulkhead should fit so tight that you have to pry it out with a small nail head.

When both bulkheads fit, cut a piece of cloth large enough to fit 2" beyond the edge of the piece all around. Line up the weave parallel to the long axis of the panel, so that it won't stretch lengthwise. Slit the cloth at the bottom and sides, and cut a V-notch into the tip.

Pencil-lining the high spots

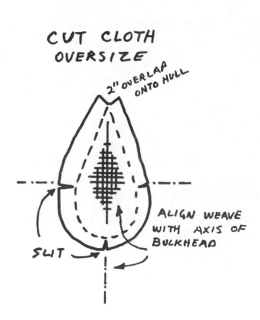

CUT CLOTH
OVERSIZE

2" OVERLAP
ONTO HULL

SLIT

ALIGN WEAVE
WITH AXIS OF
BULKHEAD

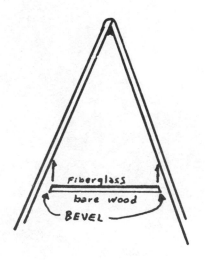

Fiberglass
bare wood
BEVEL

AIR CHAMBER
BULKHEAD —
FITTING

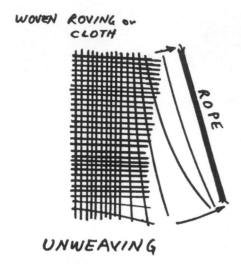

UNWEAVING

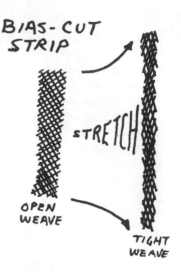

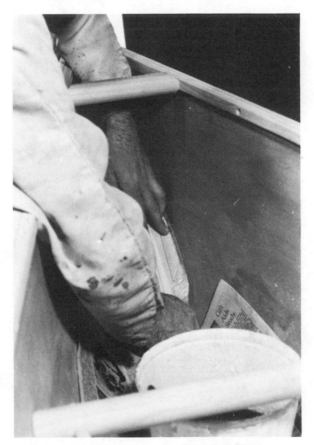

Glassing the corner with bias-cut strip

The best way to seal the corner where the bulkhead meets the boat is with a **rope** made of strands pulled from the weave of woven roving, or cloth, long enough to cover the entire perimeter of the bulkhead. As an alternate, cut narrow bias-cut strips of cloth. When stretched lengthwise, **bias-cut strips** close up their weave.

If you wish to have a permanent identification sealed under the fiberglass of your boat, prepare a **label**. Use ordinary white writing paper and typewriter, felt-tip pen, or ink pen. Some felt marker inks may dissolve in polyester. Run a test.

With 36-grit paper sand the inside of the canoe where it meets the bulkhead. Brush away dust. Insert panel in position. Lay newspaper on the floor of the canoe immediately in front of the panel. Stir surfacing wax into 4 to 6 oz. of resin, and then catalyze it.

Install Bulkhead

Paint resin onto the bulkhead and the sides of the canoe where it was sanded to accept the overlap of cloth. Stretch the bias-cut strips lengthwise, and press into the corners; or use the rope of glass strands. If using the rope, pre-saturate it on the newspaper before pressing it into the corners. A 1'' brush is about right for this job.

Overlap the rope or strips at the very top of the bulkhead. Use the brush to pat the glass into place, work out the bubbles, and saturate the glass.

Saturate the label on both sides with resin, and press it into place, squeezing out the air bubbles from behind it.

Pick up the larger cloth piece, and press it into place with the brush. Begin at the bottom and work upwards, smoothing it down. Saturate the entire piece of cloth, and get the overlap laid down smoothly on the side of the boat.

Varnish

While the resin on the bulkhead is curing, you may apply the first two coats of **varnish** to the woodwork. The thwarts and seats should be done first, and then the gunnels, so that you are not leaning over wet gunnels to do the seats. Urethane-based varnish may have its second coat applied as soon as the first coat gels to a tacky surface. These two coats should then dry overnight.

The following morning, lightly hand sand the previous coats of varnish with 100- or 150-grit. Also sand with 60-grit the cured glass stickers along the edge of the cloth overlap around the bulkheads.

Decoration

If you wish to decorate the hull with painting, apply it to the hull at this stage. Use **sign-painting enamel** and a **sign-painting quill**. The black needs to be mixed on a **palette** with a few drops of **thinner**. The palette gives better control of the amount of paint on the brush for all the colors. I have also used acrylic paint, but the enamel has "continuous ropiness" which enables me to make long, smooth edges. The quill has long, soft hairs to hold a lot of paint and follow hand movements around corners.

The Northwest Coast Indian designs that I use are best explained by Bill Holm in his book, *Northwest Coast Indian Art*, published in 1970 by the University of Washington Press as a paperback costing $4.95.

Glassing the face of the bulkhead

Northwest Coast Indian eye motif.

Eagle and frog applied around black cockpit coaming.

Heron design adapted to Kootenay stem shape

Portage straps installed with copper tacks to prevent slippage

Final Varnish

Dust off all the woodwork and the sanded area around the bulkheads. For best results use a rag lightly dampened with acetone or varnish.

Apply the third and final coat of varnish to the woodwork. Also varnish the sanded area around the bulkhead. Allow to dry for one hour or more.

Invert the boat onto two crossbars. Wipe the fiberglass exterior of the hull with acetone, removing all dust. Varnish the hull. One coat is usually sufficient to fill the sanding scratches and create a transparent finish. A satin-finish varnish will hide minor flaws and look more low-key than a gloss finish.

Seat Fabric

The seat may be webbed with a fabric that is hemmed and grommeted so that lacing may be used to tighten the seat. Use a water-repellent **canvas** that is color-fast, or **acrylic** canvas used for sail-covers. For each seat, cut the fabric to 14½" x 24" and hem the long edges. Fold 1" **webbing** into the short edge. Drive 7 **grommets** through the fabric and webbing, spacing them evenly along the edge.

Lace the fabric onto the seat bars with 1/8" **nylon cord**, about 85" long.

Portage Straps

Make the portage straps from **2" webbing**; nylon preferred over cotton. Cut two straps, 28" long, and seal the ends from fraying. Nylon can be melted together. Set two **grommets** in each end of the strap, and lace it around the portage thwarts with 35" of 1/8" **nylon cord**. Place them on the thwarts so that when the canoe is inverted and placed over your head the straps clear your ears but rest on your shoulders as close as possible to your neck. I place mine with about 7½" between the inside edges. After they are positioned correctly, use a brass or copper **tack** on one of the thwarts to hold the strap from slipping sideways.

Adding a Keel

Before you decide to add a keel, paddle without one for awhile. You may enjoy the freedom of a side slipping boat, or it may be a pain in the neck to be continually blown off course. Personally, I regard a keel as a limitation to my steering. A sturgeon-nosed Micmac canoe without a keel can follow a true course when paddled properly, but with a keel cannot easily be turned from its course. In addition, keels are treacherous rock grabbers in rivers.

If you decide to add a keel, first obtain a piece of oak or ash 16' long, ¾" wide by however deep you want it; usually ¾" to 1¼". Trim the piece to the right length, taper the ends to points, sand and varnish it. To mark the center line of the boat stretch a string from one stem to the other. Then, with a pencil, mark screw hole positions every six to eight inches alongside the string. Mark corresponding hole positions on the underside and in the center of the keel piece.

Drill the holes in the bottom of the boat to accept the shaft of a number 8 wood screw. Then tape the keel piece over the holes so that the marked positions on it line up with the holes and can be seen. Now either put the boat right side up on the floor or have someone on the other side of the bottom so you can push the drill into the keel piece without breaking the tape. Drill the holes for the wood screws. Then put a drop or two of varnish in the hole, followed by a number 8 flathead brass wood screw with a brass finishing washer under its head. Screw them down snugly and don't smash the washer by overtightening.

20' Tsunami, 18' Abenaki, and 18' Micmac ready for a cruise

Pause Before You Launch

Now that the canoe is finished, you are probably delighted and eager to launch it. Be sure you have read the page on safety and care of the boat, and make it your first responsibility to become familiar with a boat that is swamped. As you take the boat out of its enclosed space into the outdoors for the first time, notice how the size of the boat seems to change. As you begin to paddle it, remember how the boat looked and felt when it was just an idea, followed by a drawing, a set of templates occupying space, wood strips filling in that space, an empty cavity, and now something completely different as it responds to the forces acting on it, moving it through space. I am tempted to use a ritual, a launching ceremony, to express the meanings of canoe-in-water that I can grasp, as well as those I cannot. A ceremony helps to examine the questions: "What's happening with me? How do I relate to this? Am I satisfied?"

A final word of advice about paddles and paddling. I recommend that you get it together to buy a top-quality **paddle** made by Sawyer, Cadorette, or Clement. A light, rigid paddle with flawless varnish on the grips can be used endlessly with hardly any awareness that you are paddling, whereas anything less than that can make paddling a painful chore. My general rule of thumb for choosing paddle length is to pick one that is armpit height, so that the upper hand does not come above chin level during the stroke. The most efficient paddle stroke requires the upper arm to simply punch straight forward from the chin, without straining to come down from someplace over the head. However, everybody develops his own style and preference. The latest gimmick in paddles is a 5° bend at the throat. This elbow helps to utilize the energy in the last half of the stroke, where a straight-shafted paddle tends to lift the water instead of pushing it backwards. You may also wish to try a 10" wide blade instead of the standard 8", to move more water with each stroke.

Finally, to get somewhere with least effort try switching paddling sides instead of using the traditional "J" and sweep strokes. The steering strokes push the water sideways, wasting energy. It is actually faster to swing from side to side in slight arcs as you alternate paddling sides than it is to force the canoe to slide sideways a little with each stroke while believing you are traveling in the straight line of the canoe's axis! Another possible stroke is the "pitch stroke," in which the paddle blade is held at a 45° angle to the direction of the pull, in order to create a sideways steering force. Whatever you do, I hope that you will realize the paddle is an extension of your hand, just as the canoe is an extension of your body, and that anything goes when it comes to pushing and pulling on the water to get where you want to go.

J-STROKE PADDLING

SWITCH SIDES

STERNMAN CALLS "HUT!"

STRAIGHT-STROKE PADDLING

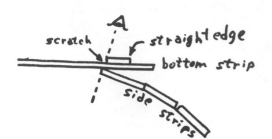

scratch   straightedge
A
bottom strip
side strips

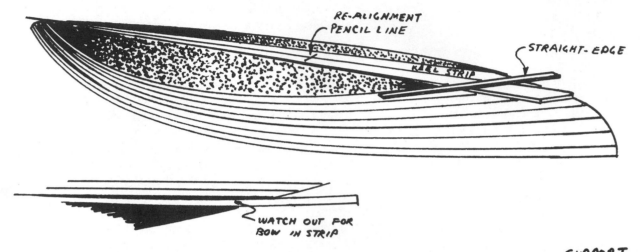

RE-ALIGNMENT
PENCIL LINE

STRAIGHT-EDGE

KEEL STRIP

WATCH OUT FOR
BOW IN STRIP

SUPPORT

TO AVOID
SPLITTING TIP

SCRATCH   WHITTLE

Planing the strip

Checking the fit

To Make a Kayak

A kayak is made in two halves, deck and hull. Both are built in similar fashion to canoe hulls. These are clamshelled together after they are glassed inside. Read the canoe instructions and become familiar with that process.

Assemble the jig for either deck or hull. Double check the length from stem to stem to make sure that it is precisely where you want it, in order to match the other half of the boat perfectly.

Stripping

Begin the stripping at the sheer line. The first strip must be perfectly level for joining to the other half. Continue stripping upwards until the stem form is almost covered with strips. Then trim off the overhanging strips, and strip the other side.

Lay a strip along the centerline of the forms and eyeball it for straightness. Staple it down. Use a knife to trim the ends to fit into the V created by the last two side strips meeting on the stem form.

Without glue, lay a strip next to the center strip. Staple it to the center form. Mark a pencil line across the two strips so that the strip can be replaced in the same position.

Mark the trim line where the bottom strip overhangs the side strip. Use a strip scrap as a straight-edge and the tip of a knife to scratch the line. The scratch line should be right on or outside of the final trim line.

Sometimes the strip has a bow in it, causing it to spring away from the strip next to it and causing an inaccurate marking of the trim line unless it is pressed flat.

Trimming Individual Strips

Break off the strip about 3 to 4 inches from the trim, and begin whittling with the knife, which should be razor-sharp. Please remember to whittle away from your hand! It is so easy to forget, and a hospital, doctor, and stitches are almost inevitable if you should slip.

As you approach the scratch line, support the narrow tip of the strip to avoid splitting it off. Finish the trim with a plane or surform tool, as you test the fit against the side strip and continue to remove wood until it fits. In the first few strips, bevel the bottom strip to meet the short face of the side strip. However, do not bevel the bottom strips after that. When the inside edges of the joint are snug and the outside edges are apart, the staple will pull the edges together and force the strips to bend together into a smooth curve.

Remove the strip after both ends are fitted, apply glue to its edge, and replace it in position. Apply glue to its joint with the side strip. Staple it to the forms with the 9/16" staples, then use the 1/4" staples to staple across the glue-lines.

As you add more strips to the bottom, the strips become shorter and the trim line will be more oblique. The fit of the bottom strip to the side strip must be snug. If it is too loose there will be dips in the hull shape between the forms, caused by "shrinking" the boat onto the forms. The last few strips to be fitted against the side strip should be marked from below with a pencil, since their joint is along a curved line, and a straight-edge is useless. The very last strip is usually very narrow and needle sharp, and it is not unusual to throw away a few mis-whittled pieces before succeeding.

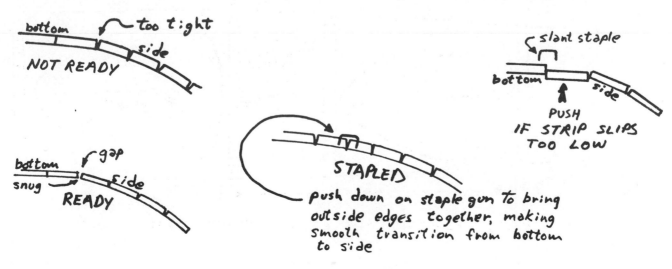

bottom — too tight / side / NOT READY

bottom — gap / snug / side / READY

STAPLED / push down on staple gun to bring outside edges together, making smooth transition from bottom to side

slant staple / bottom / side / PUSH IF STRIP SLIPS TOO LOW

Sand & Fiberglass

Allow glue to cure, pull staples, sand and fiberglass with covering coats of resin. The deck may be glassed with a single layer of 4 oz. cloth (both sides) to save weight. Thirty minutes after gel time, trim the overhanging cloth from the sheer line with a knife. Allow to cure overnight, remove from the forms, and set up forms for the other half of the kayak. Delay sanding the covering coats of resin until the boat nears completion.

The inside of the wood shell needs only disc sanding, or coarse sanding, to prepare the surface for glassing. Finish sanding is not necessary, since most of the interior will not be visible. The cockpit area of the hull may be finish sanded for looks.

Cut Cockpits

After finishing the deck, design the **cockpit cut-out templates** (p. 71) on newspaper. Fold the paper along its axis to check the symmetry. Assume the center of gravity of a person in a cockpit is about 12" in front of its rear edge, and place the cockpits so the kayak will ride level, or slightly stern heavy. Allow 48" of leg room from the back of the stern cockpit to the back of the bow cockpit. Cut the holes out of the deck with a sabre saw.

Join Top to Bottom

When both halves are complete, prepare them for joining (p. 67). Use a surform tool or coarse sandpaper wrapped around a block to cut off resin drips and cloth fragments from the sheer and to make the top edge of the sheer horizontal. Sand the interior surface of the fiberglass in a 2" wide band below the sheer to create a bonding surface for the fiberglass tape.

Place the two halves together, the deck on top, and temporarily hold in place with **masking tape**. After it has been taped in several places, check the fit all the way around the sheer line. If necessary, separate the two halves and plane or sand the high spots down. When the fit looks good, wrap tape around the bow and stern of the kayak to keep them in alignment. Then tape across the join-line very tightly at the center with **strapping tape**. Place a 6" long tape about 8" to 10" apart, alternating from side to side, and work towards the ends. Line up the edges of the sheer to be flush on the exterior of the boat. The tightness of the tape helps to hold the edges in alignment by friction. Sometimes a knife is needed to pry the edges into alignment, while somebody squeezes the boat horizontally, hugging it against their gut. As a final step, run masking tape lengthwise along the join line and around the end, to seal the resin inside.

Obtain 4 times the boat's length in **2" wide glass tape** and twice its length in **1" tape**. Glass tape is simply glass cloth woven in a narrow band. Do not use polypropylene tape for the 1" tape, because its weave becomes visible with age. It is not good on the exterior of the boat. You will need a brush on the end of a 5' to 6' **pole** to reach into the ends of the boat, a **clip-on light** to see into the ends, and a source of fresh air blowing at you.

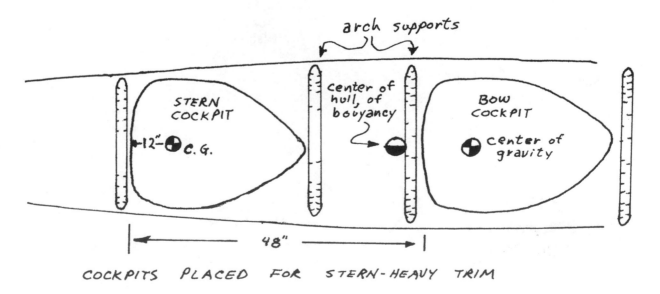

COCKPITS PLACED FOR STERN-HEAVY TRIM

Glass Tape the Join Line

Place the kayak on its edge and secure it from rolling around. Measure out two layers of the 2" tape by unrolling it onto the uppermost edge of the boat, and cut it about 4" to 6" short of the actual boat length. Use a short piece of masking tape to hold the two pieces of glass tape together at one end. Lay the two layers of glass inside the bottom edge of the boat by picking them up where they are held together and carefully feeding them through the cockpit openings and pushing them along the join-line towards the ends of the boat with a pole that has a nail in it to serve as a hook.

Catalyze 6 oz. of resin that has surfacing wax already added. Paint it onto the tape from the center towards the ends, saturating the cloth and squeezing out the air bubbles. This is done with a brush fastened to the end of a pole. Mix more resin as needed. Take care that the tape overlaps the hull and deck evenly. Allow to cure for 4 hours or more.

Rotate the kayak's non-fiberglassed sheer line down, and secure in position. Remove the masking and strapping tape from the upper sheer line. Sand a 4" wide band, 2" each side of this join-line. Dust off.

Measure off two layers of the 2" tape as before, and insert it inside the lower sheer. Measure off one layer of the 1" tape along the upper sheer, and cut off exactly at the stems.

Catalyze a small batch of resin as before. Saturate the interior layers of tape, followed by the exterior tape on the upper sheer. Cover the exterior tape with 4 coats of resin. A few drips of resin running down the hull are unavoidable, but be conservative. They will have to be sanded off later. Allow to cure for 4 hours or more.

Rotate the kayak one more time, remove the masking and strapping tape, sand the edge, and glass the remaining exterior join line with the 1" tape and 4 covering coats of resin. Wrap the stems with two layers of bias-cut patches over the join line, and cover with resin.

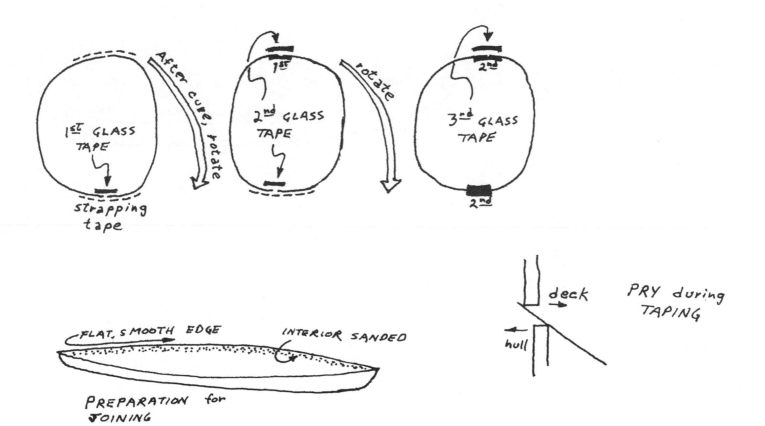

1ˢᵗ GLASS TAPE

strapping tape

After cure, rotate

2ⁿᵈ GLASS TAPE

1ˢᵗ

rotate

3ʳᵈ GLASS TAPE

2ⁿᵈ

2ⁿᵈ

FLAT, SMOOTH EDGE   INTERIOR SANDED

PREPARATION for JOINING

deck

hull

PRY during TAPING

Arch Supports

Prepare **arch supports** for the deck, fore and aft of each cockpit. Slit **cardboard tubes** in half lengthwise. Use the cores from paper towels. Slit their edges and bend them to conform to the curvature of the deck. Round off the ends so they merge with the deck just above the sheer line. Sand the inside of the deck in two 6 inch wide bands, fore and aft of each cockpit, for bonding. Dust off.

Support the kayak so that you can kneel underneath it with your head and shoulders inside the cockpit. Put the cardboard arches into place, and cut two layers of 6 oz. cloth to cover the arch and overlap onto the deck.

Presaturate the cloth layers together, on newspapers on the floor, with catalyzed resin with surfacing wax (surfacing resin). Lay the wet cloth over the cardboard tubes, and with more resin and a brush, smooth out the wrinkles and bubbles. Allow to cure.

Cockpit Coamings

On the exterior of the deck, cover with masking tape an area 4" wide around the circumference of the cockpit

Sand an area 4" around the interior of the cockpit hole. Round off the inner edge. Cut many 4" x 8" patches of bias-cut cloth, enough to cover the coaming twice. Cut enough patches of ¾" oz. **fiberglass mat** to cover the coaming once. Thus you can make a cloth-mat-cloth sandwich. If you don't want to bother with the mat, use about 4 layers of cloth or more. Obtain a **cheap vinyl garden hose**, and warm it up. Use masking tape and wood blocks to fasten it into position around the edge of the cockpit hole. Cut it to meet neatly at the apex. The hose is the mold for the coaming. Mix an **opaque pigment** in the color of your choice into one quart of resin. Lay newspapers in the bottom of the cockpit.

Catalyze a 6 oz. batch of resin. Use a brush to presaturate the cloth on the newspapers. Lay the wet cloth underneath the deck's surface and wrap it up and over the hose. Gently pull out the wrinkles. Continue around the coaming, overlapping each patch a fat inch with its neighbor. Repeat for the mat layer, and again for the cloth layer. Allow to get hard, and trim with a knife along the top of the hose. Pull the hose away from the coaming.

Apply four to five covering coats of resin to the coaming, with surfacing wax in the final coat. Allow to cure. Remove all the masking tape. Sand the coaming by hand into a smooth shape, with smooth edges and corners, and sand the inside of the deck around the cockpit.

Sand the entire exterior resin coat of the boat with disc, belt, or orbital sanders as outlined for canoe exteriors, in preparation for its finish coat of varnish.

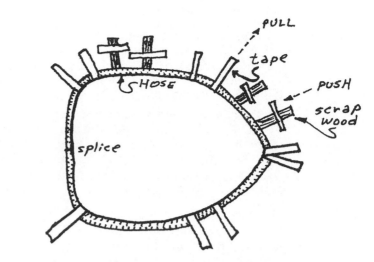

COAMING MOLD of HOSE

COAMING LAYUP

End Plugs & Flotation

Stand the kayak on its end, against a building or tree. Make a runny paste of catalyzed resin (2%) and **sanding dust** or **chopped glass fibers** (cut cloth into tiny pieces). While standing on a stool or ladder, pour the paste into the end of the boat to serve as a solid plug. Do not use 4% catalyzation since the large mass of resin will get too hot and shatter. If you are using glass fibers for the paste, use 1% catalyst. Wood dust tends to slow the catalyst down, so use more catalyst.

After the paste has gelled, mix one pint part A and one pint part B of **liquid urethane foam**, and pour into the end of the kayak for flotation. Allow to gel. Repeat for the opposite end of the boat.

Drill a hole through the tip of the boat and resin-paste plug to accommodate a **nylon rope loop**, useful for tying onto cars and for rescue.

Decide where you would like to have rope loops on the interior of the kayak for tying-in gear. Sand a small area for bonding. Use small patches of cloth or mat over part of the loop to attach them to the boat.

Seat

Design and build a **backrest and seat**. For long jaunts in a kayak it is comfortable to be able to lean back at different angles, to relieve the pressure on the buttocks. **Knee pads** under the deck and a **foot rest** help to give more control and leverage and more efficient muscle usage. I prefer the seat to be a simple pad of stiff foam rubber contact-cemented to the bottom of the boat. This keeps my center of gravity as low as possible and gives me freedom of movement very simply without a lot of hardware. However, if I sat one or two inches higher, my arms would not get so tired from paddling because they would not have to reach over the side of the boat so far.

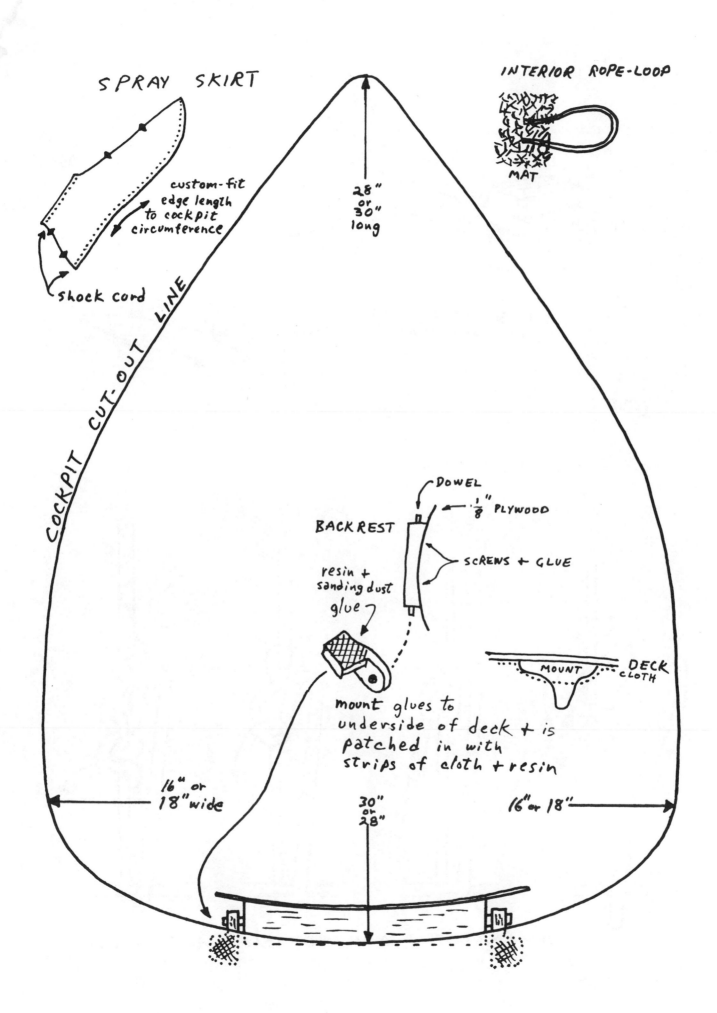

SPRAY SKIRT

custom-fit edge length to cockpit circumference

shock cord

COCKPIT CUT-OUT LINE

28" or 30" long

INTERIOR ROPE-LOOP

MAT

DOWEL

$\frac{1}{8}$" PLYWOOD

BACKREST

SCREWS + GLUE

resin + sanding dust glue

mount glues to underside of deck + is patched in with strips of cloth + resin

DECK CLOTH

MOUNT

16" or 18" wide

30" or 28"

16" or 18"

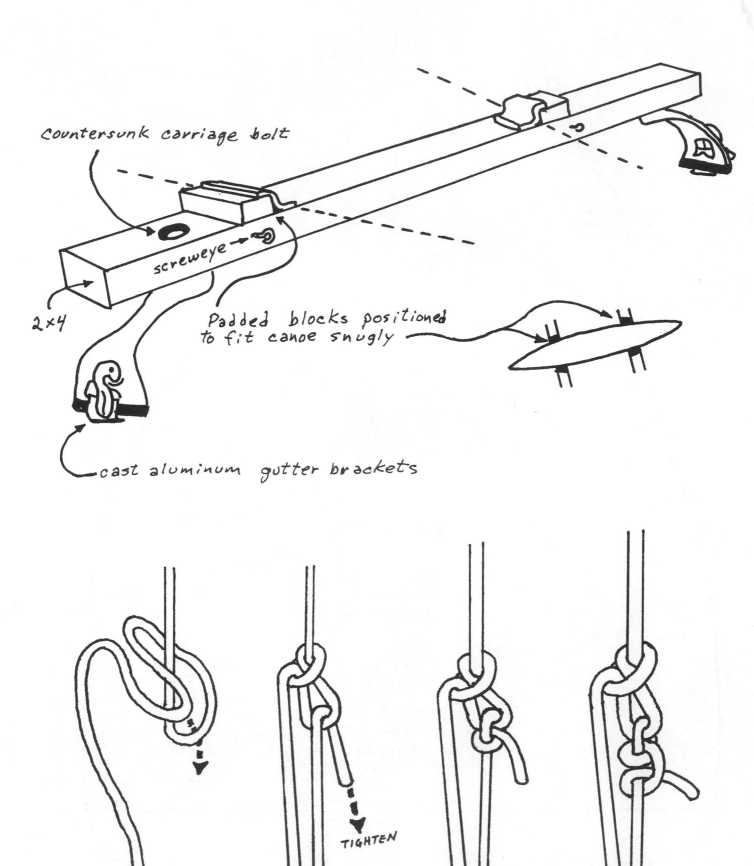

Countersunk carriage bolt

screweye

2×4

Padded blocks positioned to fit canoe snugly

cast aluminum gutter brackets

TIGHTEN

SLIP-KNOT   AND   DOUBLE HALF-HITCH

Car Top Carriers

When your boat is on top of your car, it is not only a wind-catching sail for head-winds and side-winds, it is also a potential missile should it come loose during sudden stops or collisions.

For cars without rain gutters or for extreme simplicity, there are several manufacturers of snap-on gunnel cushions which permit the gunnels to ride directly on the roof of the car. This arrangement requires enough rope tie-downs to prevent the canoe from sliding around on the roof, sideways as well as front-to-back. Suction-cup style racks with adjustable webbing are not recommended. They are just too flimsy. The rack which I use and recommend is made of a 2 x 4 and a set of cast aluminum gutter brackets (Model UKS-1, Quik-N-Easy Products, Monrovia, California). These brackets grip gutters securely to prevent slipping.

Since I only use my rack for carrying my canoe, I have blocks mounted on the bars to act as stops. When the canoe is tied securely between 4 of these blocks on the two bars, almost all possible movement is eliminated. I have padded the block and bar with dense foam rubber covered with a reinforced vinyl to prevent wear and tear on the gunnels.

Kayaks are a special problem, especially the 18' and 20' boats included in this book. Shaped and padded wooden blocks or webbing slung between two uprights are necessary to cradle the boat.

For tying the canoe to the carrier bars I have installed screw-eyes in front of the blocks and then stretched a thick, 31 to 36" rubber tarp tie-down over the canoe from one eye to the other. Tarp tie-downs are available at truck-stops and some auto-supply stores. Bicycle inner tubes may also be used this way.

Be very careful when stretching and releasing these straps because the metal S-hook is usually headed straight for your or your buddy's face when they slip out of your hands.

The bow and stern of the boat should also be tied to the outside corners of the bumpers, using at least a 1/4" diameter nylon rope. Tie the middle of the rope to the rope loop or closest thwart of the canoe with a double or half hitch so that the rope will not slip back and forth. Then tie each end of the rope to the outside ends of the bumpers to form a triangle with the rope. A taut line hitch can be tightened to take up slack without retying and holds firm under tension. Illustrated

is an alternate which allows you to leave a loop permanently in the rope for repeated use.

To prevent the bumper edge from cutting the rope, either purchase molded polyethylene bumper hooks or install an eyebolt through the bumper with a nut and lock-washer.

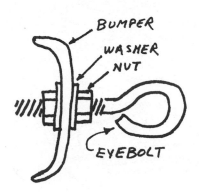

While on trips with the boat, check the ropes and carrier every morning and every time you stop for gas. If one of the ropes breaks or comes loose, will the remaining ropes be able to hold the canoe until a safe stop can be made?

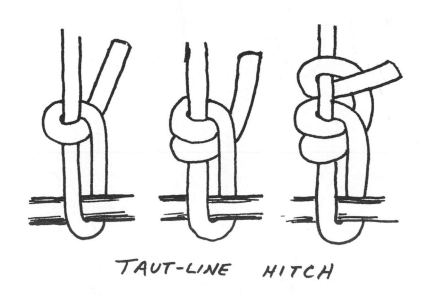

TAUT-LINE HITCH

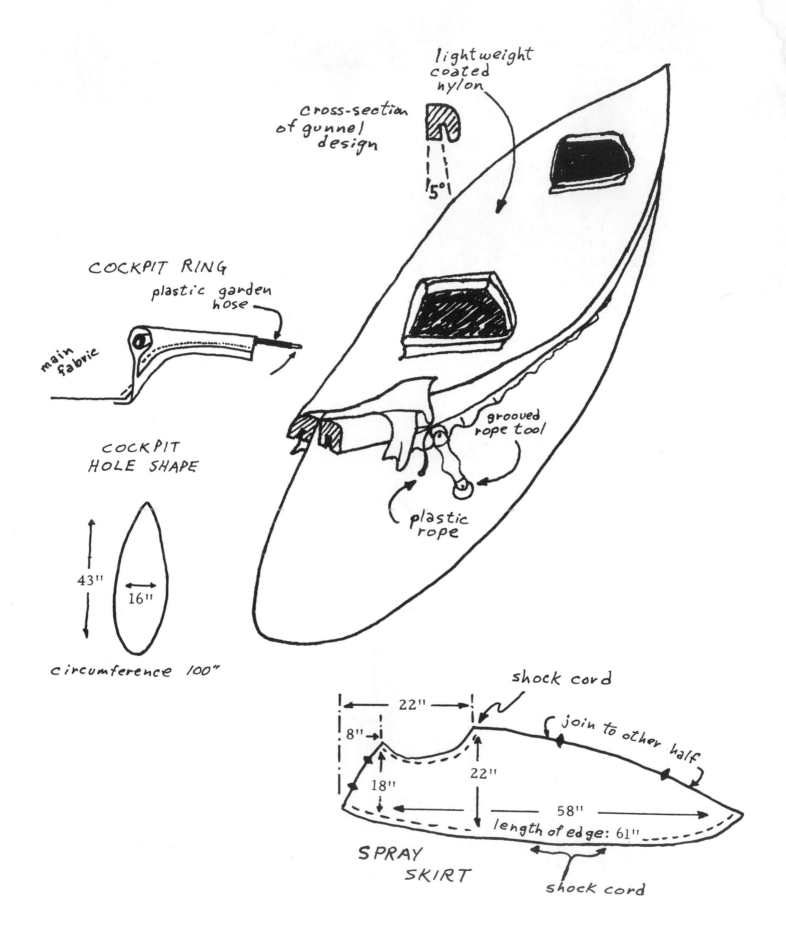

lightweight coated nylon

cross-section of gunnel design

5°

COCKPIT RING

plastic garden hose

main fabric

COCKPIT HOLE SHAPE

43"

16"

circumference 100"

grooved rope tool

plastic rope

shock cord

22"

8"

join to other half

22"

18"

58"

length of edge: 61"

SPRAY SKIRT

shock cord

Canoe Cover

The cover I have presented here is very simple to make and is very watertight in heavy water. It is almost as easy to put onto the canoe as snaps, and much faster to take off. My experience with snap fasteners has been: (1) Put them below the gunnel, or you will continually be hitting your thumb on them while paddling; (2) in plunging through heavy waves, much water will surge upwards between the snaps, into the boat, unless waterproof tape is run the length of the cover's edge. Tape, however is expensive and ugly.

It helps a lot to decide whether or not you want a cover before you build your boat, because your decision affects the design of the gunnel. The gunnel needs to have a slot cut into it with a table saw set at a five degree pitch, with a blade one eighth inch thick. This slot is for accepting a plastic rope that can be bought at hardware stores and is used for installing window screens into aluminum frames. It is used in the same way here. The fabric is held over the slot and the grooved rope tool is used to push the rope and fabric up into the slot. Here it is held by friction until you grab the end of the rope and unzip the whole cover in a flash. The five degree angle to the slot allows you to get your hand around the rope tool when it is right up against the side of the canoe.

The best thing for making a canoe cover is a lightweight coated nylon. You might be able to buy surplus or remnants from a raincoat manufacturer or discount yardage store.

To mark the boat on the fabric, simply tape the fabric over the canoe and use a marker to draw a line about 3 inches below the gunnel so that there is enough excess fabric to push into the slot. Mark the position of the seats by untaping a little of the fabric so you can peek under it. The cockpit hole should begin about four inches behind the rear bar of the seat and extend 43 inches forward in a pumpkin seed shape. Use a 100 inch string to get the right circumference to match the spray skirt.

Cut a strip of fabric about 6 inches wide and 100 inches long to fit the circumference of the hole you have cut for the cockpit. Sew one edge of it around a hoop of plastic garden hose the same length. Then sew it to the main fabric. You will have to force it into a sharp bend at the forward end of the cockpit. That finishes the main cover and all the remains is the making of two spray skirts.

The spray skirt is made in two halves, left and right. Follow the illustration when laying out the pattern on some sheets of newspaper taped together. Use a string 61 inches long to create the right length edge. The shock cord that gets hemmed into the edge has to be shorter in order to create grip on the cockpit ring and seal it tight, yet allow it to be yanked off in emergencies. Experiment to find the right length. The shock cord around your chest should be snug but not tight, or else it will hurt. Having it up around your lower chest helps splashes to run off instead of forming a puddle in your lap. Suspenders are necessary to keep it up there because the natural tendency of the shock cord is to slide down to your hips unless you have the jolly fortune of a pregnancy or a beer belly to hold it up.

The spray skirt may look funny on you men before you get into the canoe, but that is when you put it on — before. After you are seated in the canoe and the nervous tension about shooting the rapids has begun to build, you have to remain calm to stretch the skirt over the ring. Hook the shockcord under the cockpit ring behind your back. Then work both hands forward on both sides simultaneously, hooking the shock cord over the ring. With one final long-reaching tug, pop it over the front. You could try it reverse fashion, ending in back where you can't see your hands. It might work better for you.

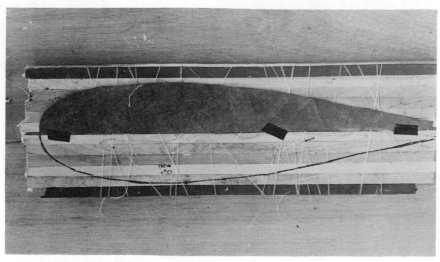

Marking outline of blade shape on blade. Pattern has been turned over and other half of blade is about to be marked.

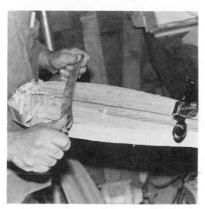

Beginning to remove wood from blade with drawknife; spokeshave is resting on blade.

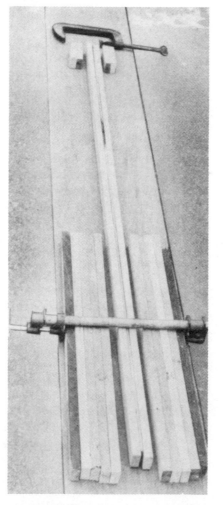

The blade handle and shaft have been assembled, and are ready to be glued together. At least three clamps will be needed for the blade assembly to insure a uniform glue line.

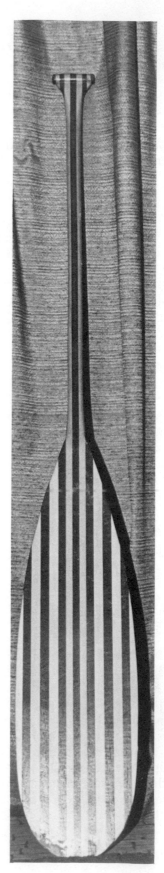

The finished product.

Make Your Own Canoe Paddle

Reprinted from "Wilderness Camping", Vol.5, 1975. With the kind permission of the author L.W. (Jack) Davis.

On first thought, it doesn't seem possible to build a paddle that would be good enough to propel a canoe. Once you try it, though, you'll find paddle-making a most satisfying and useful venture.

The only materials you'll need are wood and glue. A two-part, waterproof resorcinol glue is probably the best. Next would be a phenolic resin glue such as Weldwood. My next choice is an aliphatic glue (Titebond), made by Franklin.

A good paddle is laminated from strips of wood to help prevent warping or splitting. Most any softwood except yellow pine works well. Lightweight hardwoods such as yellow poplar also are acceptable. Any width of strip can be used for the blade of the paddle. Thinner strips make better paddles, but more glue is necessary.

Decide upon the dimensions of the paddle you want—its length, and the length and width of its blade. A blade 26 to 28 inches long is about average. Strips for the blade are usually made about 3/4" wide by 1¼" thick. An easy way to make good strips is to rip them from a planed 3/4" board.

The center section can be made of one piece of wood, but my preference is to use three pieces. The center piece is hardwood (ash, hickory, oak, maple or beech) and is 1/4" thick, more or less. The other two pieces are 1/2" thick. When these three pieces are glued up, a 1¼" square piece results.

Do the gluing in two stages. First glue and clamp the pieces that make up the center section. Then glue and clamp the strips that make up each side of the blade, and each side of the grip, separately. When the glue has set up, remove the clamps.

Next, apply glue to one side of each of the glue-up pieces that make up the blade, position these on the long center piece, position the clamps and tighten them. Do the same with the two small pieces that make up the grip.

Now outline the shape of the blade on kraft paper, grocery bag paper or newspaper. Fold it in half lengthwise and cut it in half. Place the best half in the exact center of the blade and tape it down on the straight side. Trace around the curved edge. Remove the tape, flip the pattern, fasten it down again (lining up the end marks), and trace around the curved edge as before. If you're not satisfied, retrace it **now**. Don't try to nibble away at it with a wood rasp later.

Cut away the wood up to the traced line with a sabre saw or jig saw, band saw, coping saw, drawknife or rasp. Similarly, trace an outline on the grip and remove the rough wood. The rough shaping is now completed, except for the handle.

Draw lines about 3/8" in from both sides of the four corners on the handle. Use a cheap, school-type compass to draw these. Fasten the pencil in the compass so that it is about 1/4" up from the point. Let the point ride over the edge as you draw it along the side from grip to blade.

Remove the wood up to the drawn lines with a rasp or spokeshave. Now you'll have a fairly uniform octagon; rounding this off is easy. Use a rasp or spokeshave first, and follow this with a piece of sandpaper or emery cloth about 3" x 12" in size. Use the sandpaper as though you were shining shoes. Occasionally shift the position of the cloth and check the handle for high spots. It's much easier to shape the handle, grip and blade when the paddle is held firmly in a vise or held down to a table.

Most of the wood can be removed from the blade and grip with a rasp, spokeshave, or drawknife. When the shape is about right, go to a finer file or sandpaper and finish with this. An orbital sander is useful for final shaping and sanding of the blade.

The shape of the grip is up to you. I prefer a modified pear grip; WC's editor opts for a full T-handle. Both are more difficult to form than the conventional pear.

Blade cross-section is also a matter of preference. The blade may taper from the center to each edge and from the upper end to the tip; it may taper from the upper end to the tip, but with parallel opposite sides. I like the latter, because the edges of the paddle are a little thicker and less prone to breakage. And those flat sides make a good surface for filleting fish in wild places where flat surfaces are rare.

The finished paddle must be coated to protect it. Give it a coat of thinned varnish to fill the pores in the wood, sand lightly, and finish with two or three coats of varnish, again sanding lightly between coats. Use marine-grade spar varnish or **exterior** polyurethane only.

[I've found that spar varnish will soften on a warm day, while polyurethane stays hard and smooth. HNR]

Gluing Notes:

Strips to be glued should have parallel sides and should be free of oil, paint, varnish and dirt.

When gluing pieces together, it is usually necessary to put glue on only one piece, but be sure you apply enough so a little will squeeze out when clamps are tightened.

Clamps are expensive, and there are substitutes. Fasten 2 x 2's or 2 x 4's to your workbench; space them far enough apart so the pieces lie between them with about 1/2" to spare. Wooden wedges driven in the ends and top will hold the pieces securely.

You can also cut a strip of rubber about 1/2" wide and several feet long from a discarded truck innertube and wrap it tightly around and around the pieces all along their length.

While all glues are somewhat fussy about temperature, the two-component resorcinols are the fussiest by far. Read the instructions on the container and follow them without deviation.

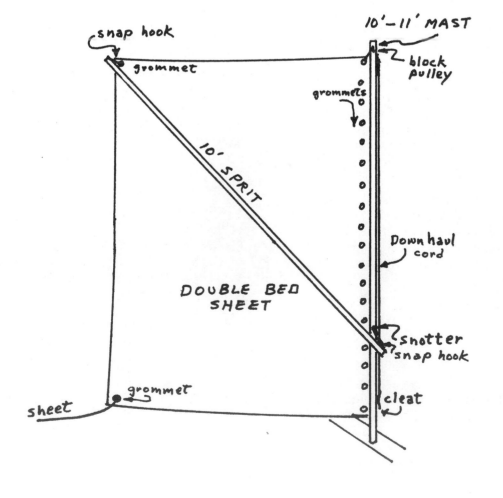

Canoe Sailing

I have never sailed a canoe myself, although I intend to do it soon. The information presented here has been selected from back issues of canoeing magazines, which I have footnoted below. This article covers some of the pleasures of sailing, the design of the equipment from simple to more complex, and the fundamentals of technique.

Sailing is exciting and takes little physical effort once your sail is set. It does require some mental alertness and good judgment in order to stay dry, however.

"I would rather sail a canoe than paddle one. Very few who have canoes realize that one can sail even a large canoe all alone on a large lake or a bay and have fun while doing it under adverse conditions where two canoeists paddling there would be having a rough time of it.

"I do not wish to mislead anyone to think that I've never been scared at times. But this holds true when traveling in any small boat if you travel very far in one. These close shaves that may seem like a normal course of events at first seldom materialize as you gain experience, for you have learned to keep a few steps ahead of trouble.

"If I plan to sail in a large body of water, I not only carry and wear a life preserver but also wedge an inflated inner tube under both canoe seats—for I've learned from experience that I am not able to shake out a canoe to get it dry in our choppy waters, especially with sailing gear on board.

"Sailing is as easy as paddling. One can get the basic idea in twenty minutes. . . . There is really very little to it. That's the trouble. It takes very little time for the newcomer to become competent under ideal conditions. But what takes time is to acquire seamanship —that combination of common sense, knowledge and experience which gives ability not only to get out of difficult situations, but, most important, to avoid getting into them in the first place."[1]

Equipment

Canoe sailing rigs need to be simple, compact, and light. The sail must be easily raised and lowered while on the water and stowed where it will not interfere with paddling. For the be-ginner, the sail design should have a low center of effort (the geometrically central point of the wind's pushing) for stability, a modest sail area of 30 to 55 square feet, and be economical and easy to build.

The simplest rig possible to meet these requirements is the bed-sheet sail.

"Yes, my sail is a Sears and Roebuck best Perma Prest **double bed sheet**. It is inexpensive, easily obtainable, requires no sewing, and meets all the criteria I have enumerated. (A white bed sheet also makes an excellent awning in a hot, sunny camp far from shade trees.) For the more daring, they are available in gay colored prints. The size, about 55 square feet, seems about right to me. One could, of course, go to single or king size. Grommets are needed at each corner and along the luff spaced about one foot apart. The sail is held to the mast by halyard and downhaul and by short laces tied to pairs of adjacent grommets and passing around the mast.

"The mast is ten to eleven feet long, unstayed, and stepped behind the bow seat where it does not interfere with the bow paddler. A ten-foot-long sprit (a wooden [or bamboo] pole about one and one-quarter inches in diameter) is fastened between the after peak of the sail and the snotter (a loop of line looped around the mast in a Prusik knot which can be slipped along the mast to adjust the position of the sprit). The sail is sheeted by a line tied to the grommet in the after end of the foot and passing through a block fastened at the stern and then to a cam cleat. The lack of a boom means the foot of the sail can be at gunwale height, which helps in keeping the center of effort low. The sail can be quickly reefed to half area by removing the sprit. The sprit must be unfastened from the snotter when the sail is raised or lowered, and I use small snap hooks at each end of the sprit for convenience.

"This bed sheet rig has proven itself in a twenty-mile open-water voyage to the southern tip of Tiburon Island in the Sea of Cortez with 10-knot winds and four-foot breaking seas. The return trip was made in light winds by alternately paddling, sailing, and then both simultaneously."[2]

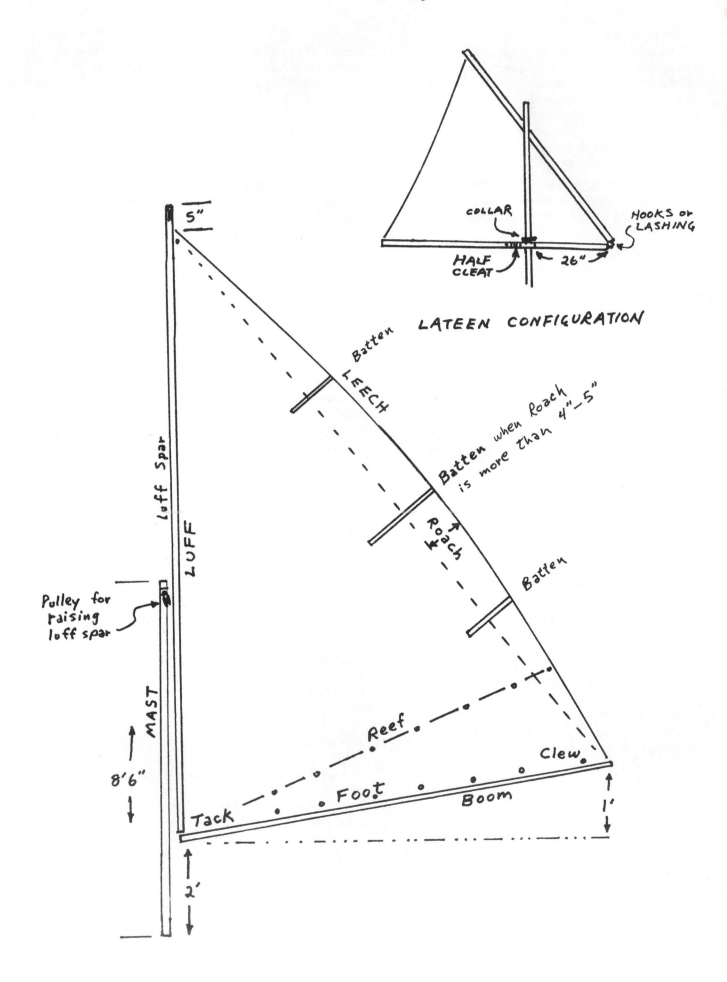

LATEEN CONFIGURATION

The mast may be constructed of wood or aluminum tubing. If made of wood, a 2" diameter at the foot seems best, and it may taper to 1¼" at the top. Aluminum tubing should be .058 wall, Spec. 6061T6, and 2" in diameter for everything except sails having less than 40 square feet in area. Spars, sprits, or booms may be about 1/2" to 3/4" smaller than the mast.

Masts are held in place with a mast thwart behind the bow seat, placed so that the belly of the sail is positioned over the widest part of the boat. This is called "placing the center of effort over the center of lateral resistance" and helps the boat to stay on course without a lot of correction and drag from rudder and leeboards. The mast thwart must be sturdy, ranging in dimension from 1 x 4 to 2 x 4, depending on the material it is made of. The hole for the mast may be bored through the thwart's center or a cleat or strap may be fastened to the thwart's stern edge, preserving the integrity of the wood.

A socket or step must be fastened to the bottom of the boat directly underneath or slightly ahead of the hole in the mast thwart. Moving it ahead gives the mast slight "rake" into the wind.

Triangular sails used with a tall luff spar enable one to lower the sail without unstepping the mast or standing up in the canoe. The mast is 8'6" tall with a small pulley placed about 3" from the top. The luff spar is raised and lowered by means of a rope passed through the pulley. I have listed here three sizes of triangular sails.[3]

1. 46 square feet, luff spar 11'7½", boom 8'. Sail: luff 11'2½", leech 12'8", roach 9", foot 7'7".

2. 58 square feet, luff spar 12', boom 9'6". Sail: luff 11'10", leech 13'10", roach 5", foot 8'10".

3. 65 square feet, luff spar 13'6", boom 9'9". Sail: luff 12'7½", leech 14'9", roach 4", foot 9'3½". This sail takes a mast 9'9" tall.

Reefing the sail makes it into a lateen configuration.

"The regular boom jaw is released from the mast and the boom slides forward to engage a lateen jaw placed on the boom 26 inches aft of the main boom jaw. The reef line is a small continuous braided nylon line passing through the reef grommets in the foot of the sail below. Beginning at the clew, the reef line is drawn tight with the surplus line being fastened to a cleat located near the tack on the boom jaw. Reef grommets are 3'4" above the clew, going diagonally down to tack grommets, and are in line with the grommets in the foot of the sail. Rather than lacing a sail to the spars, use nylon sail clasps which the Alcort popularized on their Sailfish these past few years."[3]

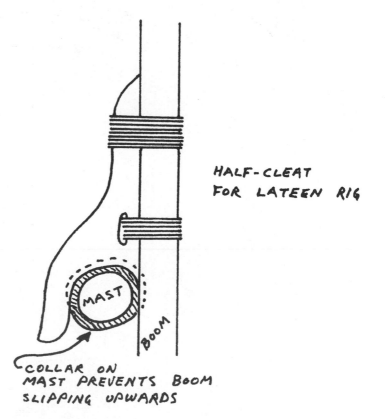

HALF-CLEAT FOR LATEEN RIG

MAST

BOOM

COLLAR ON MAST PREVENTS BOOM SLIPPING UPWARDS

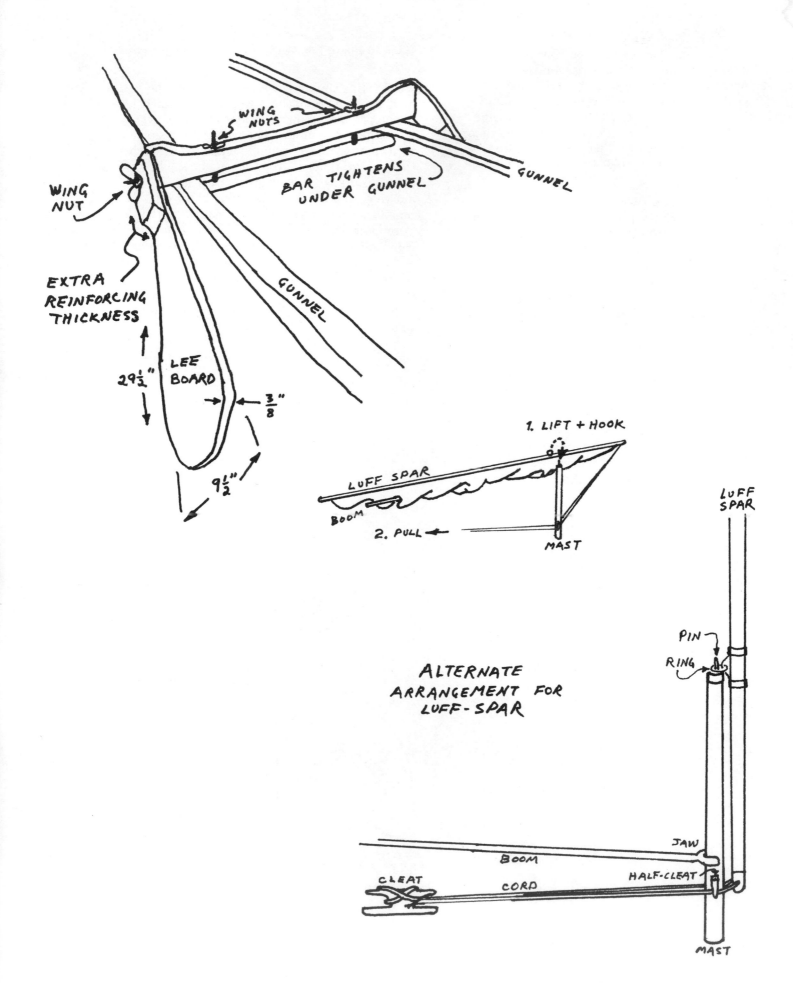

WING
NUTS

BAR TIGHTENS
UNDER GUNNEL

GUNNEL

WING
NUT

EXTRA
REINFORCING
THICKNESS

GUNNEL

$29\frac{1}{2}$"

LEE
BOARD

$\frac{3}{8}$"

$9\frac{1}{2}$"

1. LIFT + HOOK

LUFF SPAR

BOOM

2. PULL ←

MAST

ALTERNATE
ARRANGEMENT FOR
LUFF-SPAR

LUFF
SPAR

PIN

RING

JAW

BOOM

HALF-CLEAT

CLEAT

CORD

MAST

To make your own sail, sidestepping the professional sailmaker, this is the only advice I could find, from 1882:

". . . There is no better material than unbleached twilled cotton sheeting. It is to be had two and a half or even three yards wide. In cutting out your sail, let the selvedge be at the 'leech,' or aftermost edge. This, of course, makes it necessary to cut the luff and foot 'bias,' and they are very likely to stretch in the making, so that the sail will assume a different shape from what was intended. To avoid this, baste the hem carefully before sewing and 'hold in' a little to prevent fulling. It is a good plan to tack the material on the floor before cutting and mark the outline of the sail with a pencil. Stout tape stitched along the bias edges will make a sure thing of it, and the material can be cut, making due allowance for the hem. Better take feminine advice on this process. The hems should be half an inch deep all around, selvedge and all, and it will do no harm to reinforce them with cord if you wish to make a thoroughly good piece of work."[4]

And here is some advice for making a rudder and leeboards:

"Our rudder, of one quarter inch plywood, is made so that it engages the water from one to two feet behind the canoe and to a depth of just a little deeper than the keel line. It is hinged to the stern of the canoe in such a way that the pin can be pulled and the rudder removed. There is a crosspiece at the top of the rudder 14" long. The rudder is moved by a rope which is attached to each end of this crosspiece and goes through two eyes on each side of the canoe and two pulleys—one at each end of the main thwart.

"Our leeboards are from a sailing outfit for a Klepper folding boat. They are made of 3/8" plywood, 9½" wide at the lower end and 29½" long over all. They are attached to a crosspiece by means of a bolt and wing nut through a hole 27" up from the bottom of each board. They can be tightened at any angle. The whole assembly is lashed to the thwart just aft of the bow seat."[5]

So, once you have made all these pieces of equipment and figured out the niceties of fitting them to your boat, you are almost ready to hit the water. A few extra features not mentioned thus far are (1) a quick-release swivel cleat for the main sheet, (2) a cleat to wrap the downhaul around so the luff spar stays up, (3) "a collar on the lower mast so that the boom, when once in position, cannot slip upward and suffer the sail to bag,"[4] and (4) a hook or simple lashing at the junction of the boom and luff spar, "having sufficient play to allow the two spars to shut up together like a pair of dividers."[4] One more last thing: a bailing bucket made from a plastic gallon jug with its bottom cut off.

Technique

"Make your first practical experiment with a small sail and with the wind blowing toward the shore. Row out a little way, and then sail in any direction in which you can make the boat go, straight back to shore if you can, with the sail out nearly at right angles with

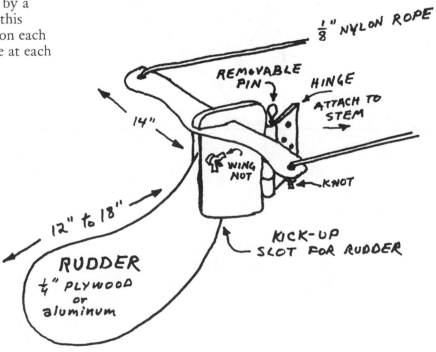

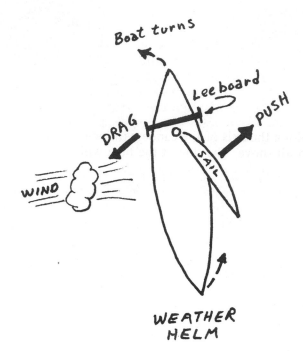

WEATHER
HELM

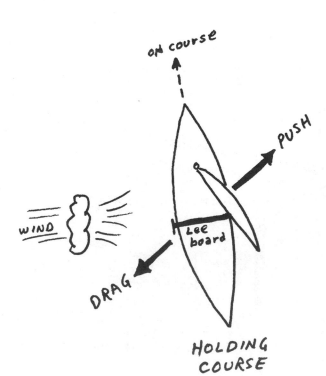

HOLDING
COURSE

the boat. Then try running along shore with the sheet hauled in a little and the sail on the side nearest the shore. You will soon learn what your craft can do and will probably find that she will make very little, if any, headway to windward. This is partly because she slides sidewise over the water. To prevent it you may use a 'leeboard'. . . . It should be placed a little forward of the middle of the boat. It must be on the side away from the wind—the lee side. In making a landing, always calculate to have the boat's head as near the wind as possible when she ceases to move."[4]

"One of the best ways to really learn open canoe sailing is to sail one without a rudder—using just a steering paddle. This teaches one a lot about the way a canoe likes to be sailed. . . . The rudder provides such an easy control that it can obscure a lot of mistakes about the position of your leeboards and those mistakes can induce unnecessary rudder drag, this being one of many.

"Using a paddle for steering teaches immediately that the farther forward the leeboards are placed, the greater the weather helm (the tendency the canoe has to round up into the wind), and likewise the farther forward you place your own weight, the greater the tendency to weather helm, and, of course, the obverse is also true. The farther aft the sailor's weight is, the less the weather helm.

"Sailing before the wind, for instance, with the leeboards fully retracted and without a rudder, in most canoes one may have to sit all the way back on the stern deck to avoid slowing the canoe down—through excessive use of the steering paddle. When trying to learn to sail a canoe without a rudder, one should use a sail with a small sail area. . . ."[1]

1. "Some Thoughts on Sailing a Canoe," by Norris Van Gilderen, Vol. 5, No. 2, USCA *Canoe News,* Summer 1972.
2. "The 'Bed-Sheet' Sail," by Cecil Carnes, Jr., Vol. 32, No. 6, *American Canoeist,* Dec. 1972.
3. "Canoe Sails," by Norris Van Gilderen, Vol. 5, No. 3, USCA *Canoe News,* Fall 1972.
4. "How to Rig and Sail Small Boats," by Charles L. Norton, in *The American Boy's Handy Book,* Charles Scribner's Sons, 1882.
5. "Sailing Equipment for a Canoe," by Eric Oxelson, Vol. 6, No. 9, Minnesota Canoe Association *Hut!,* August 1972.

Living With It

Safety

The best safety factor is Experience, so develop your skill by using your boat in a wide variety of conditions. Be cautious when going beyond your ability. If you have any doubts about your swimming ability, take lessons and wear a lifejacket until you are a strong swimmer. Always wear a lifejacket when paddling in cold, moving, or large bodies of water. When running rough rivers or ocean, it is best to add additional flotation by securely tying in a couple of inner tubes. Also tie a line 25 feet or longer with a float on the end of it to each end of the boat. Leave it loose so you can grab it when swamped.

Your very first order of business after receiving your boat is to become familiar with your boat when it is overturned or swamped. Get a healthy respect for the weight of water and the amount of time and energy it takes to self-rescue a canoe.

Self-Rescue

The following assumes that you are too far from shore or other boats to swim and pull the swamped boat to safety.

1. Stay with the boat. Make sure your partner is OK. Get your lifejacket on immediately if you do not have it on already. If in a stream, move to the upstream end of the boat and float with your feet downstream.

2. Relax and plot your strategy. If the water is numbing cold or bad rapids or falls are ahead, you do not have time to rescue the boat. Forget the boat and save your life. Head for shore.

3. Fastest way to empty the boat is to turn it keel up, trapping a large air pocket under it. Swim under the gunnel and up inside into the air pocket. Two people can then lift one gunnel out of the water to break the suction, and then throw the boat clear of the water with a flip to the side. It should land keel down with only a few gallons of water in it. Naturally, pushing up on the boat will push you under, so a lifejacket will help. Consult the Red Cross book, *Canoeing*, for instructions on climbing back into the boat.

4. Second best way to empty the boat is to turn it on its side, so that the thwarts are vertical. The boat will float half submerged, with its stems about even with the water. Push down on one stem slightly and push that stem along the axis of the canoe with one mammoth shove. The side of the boat will act as a plane to push the boat higher. Most of the water will slide out of the rear. The motion should end with the canoe falling keel down with several gallons of water in it.

Deliberately swamp the boat several times and practice these techniques until you can do them fully clothed in cold water.

Storage & Varnish

Your worst enemy is exposure to ultraviolet light, so choose a shaded place. If stored outdoors, tie the boat down to prevent storm winds from blowing it away. When it becomes necessary to refinish the boat because of wear or scratches, sand all the woodwork and the exterior of the hull with 100-grit sandpaper, and paint with one quart of urethane varnish. The varnish will fill and blend the scratches in the fiberglass, making it transparent again.

Beaching

Your boat can support a large load when it has a cushion of water to distribute the weight. Do not load or step into any boat when all or part of it is supported by land. When in shallow water, do not hesitate to get your feet wet to protect your boat. Loading a canoe is most easily done by two people, one holding the boat while the other puts in the gear and then sits in the boat. Then the remaining person puts one foot in the boat and pushes off with the other foot.

In order to enter or exit from a kayak, support your weight on your hands, placing one on the middle of the deck immediately behind the cockpit and placing the other on the shaft of the paddle, which has been placed diagonally across the deck into shallow water or shore, creating a stable outrigger. Insert your feet into the cockpit, then lift your hips up and over the cockpit coaming.

Portage

One person can carry the canoe inverted with the portage yoke over his head. To lift the canoe up, stand the canoe on its side, bringing your knees against the bottom in the middle. Pick the canoe up onto the top of your legs with one hand on each gunnel. Use the weight of your hips to throw the canoe up and out in an arc which ends with the canoe over your head.

The short thwart near the ends may be used for a two-person carry. Do not strain the canoe by carrying it loaded with gear. Do not sit on the thwarts, sit on the seats.

Repairs

If you have a crack, cut, break, or rupture in the shell of your boat, inspect it closely to determine the extent of the damage. If it is only a bruise or scratch, it probably does not need repair. Check the watertightness by pushing the area with your finger and watch for water and bubbles moving under the fiberglass. It may also feel spongy. If the wood is wet, it needs new fiberglass.

A gouge through the outside layer of cloth into the wood which does not go all the way through the wood may be filled with a paste mixture of catalyzed resin (use 4% catalyst) and fine sanding dust. Cover with the cloth patch before the paste mixture gels.

To repair clean breaks in the hull which break all layers of glass and wood, simply push the wood back into place, strip away loose glass on both sides of the wood, and proceed from step #1. However, on the inside of the hull, no extra covering coats or varnish are needed.

1. Shove a chisel into the cut, and, by prying and pushing, remove all the loose fiberglass and uncover the wet parts of the wood. If it is a fresh puncture, you may only have to remove the glass about 1" or so back from the cut. Old punctures will have absorbed more moisture along the grain of the wood, necessitating the removal of glass up to 6" away from the original cut. Do not be afraid to remove too much material. It is all going to be covered with new glass cloth anyway, and imprisoning moisture in the wood may cause you to do the patch all over again. Use the chisel with the beveled nose against the wood. This prevents excessive gouging and lifting of glass.

2. With rough 36-grit sandpaper, sand the area 3" around the opening you have made and feather the edge of the glass into the wood. As you do this, you may notice parts of the edge

lifting up as you pass over them—they are still loose. Cut some more with the chisel, sand some more, etc. Finish with 60- and 100-grit sandpaper.

3. Allow to dry in a warm place overnight. If possible use a heat lamp or sunlight, until there is not any possibility of moisture remaining in the wood.

4. Clean off dust. Paint with three coats of clear lacquer, if possible a sanding sealer lacquer. Allow time to dry between coats, and sand lightly after each coat is dry. This primer coat is only necessary over cedar, not spruce. If in doubt, do it.

5. Cut a patch of 6 oz. cloth 2" larger than the hole to make a single layer on the sides, double layer on the bottom.

6. Catalyze a small amount of "surfacing polyester resin" with 1% catalyst in warm weather, 2% in cool weather. Lay the patch over the hole, paint with resin, using either a brush or a squeegee made of cardboard. Squeeze out all the air bubbles trapped in the cloth. Allow to gel. Clean out your brush in acetone before it gels.

7. On the exterior of the boat, paint on 3 more coats of resin immediately after the preceding coat has gelled. This fills in the texture of the cloth and makes a bulk of resin which can be sanded smooth and fair.

8. Allow to cure overnight.

9. Sand the covering coats of resin smooth and flat to a fair curve with the rest of the hull, using 60-grit paper followed by 100-grit. Do not be concerned if you sand into the edge of the patch, as this is necessary to feather the edge.

10. Varnish with satin finish urethane varnish.

To repair "messy" ruptures where it is necessary to replace wood strips, obtain strips to match the original dimensions and color as closely as possible. Trim off the shattered wood until you have solid wood. Trim the new strips to fit. Glue them into position holding them with tape, staples, or clamps until the glue is cured. Then sand the wood flat and smooth to match the original curve of the hull.

Emergency repairs in the woods. Minor breaks and cuts can be sealed with a waterproof cloth adhesive tape. Large breaks may be filled with 2 or 3 layers of fiberglass cloth painted with resin. Support the cloth until it gels hard with a mound of dirt, large rock, piece of wood, milk carton, cardboard, etc. In cool weather, it will be necessary to warm the boat with a large reflector fire.

Death and Departure

When the time comes, don't forget to say
goodbye. Clean up your relationship with the
boat, and don't leave things hanging, unsaid.
Speak about the bad times as well as the
good. Tell the boat what's happening with
you, and wish its molecules an even better
assembly next time. Cremate the remains,
and celebrate new beginnings with a party.

A man is part of his canoe and all it knows

Information on canoeing and kayaking activities, magazines and books can be obtained from:

American Canoe Association
4260 East Evans Avenue
Denver, Colorado, 80222

United States Canoe Association
c/o E. Heinz Wahl
1818 Kensington Blvd.
Fort Wayne, Indiana 46805

Information on pre-built and built-to-order strip canoes and materials can be obtained from:

Wilderness Boats, Inc.
Rte. 1, Box 101A
Carlton, Oregon 97111

Any clarification or information you might want from me, or feedback you wish to offer, please write c/o the publisher:
David Hazen
c/o Tamal Vista Publications
547 Howard Street
San Francisco, California 94105

Catalyst Chart

**RECOMMENDED MEKP CATALYST
RATES FOR MOST RESINS:**

Temperatures (Degrees F.)	Percentages
90	.5%
85	.75%
75	1.0%
70	1.5%
65	2.0%

CATALYST AMOUNT
in cubic centimeters (cc)

CATALYZATION RATE

OUNCES OF RESIN	0.25%	0.5%	1%	2%	3%	4%
2	0.2	0.3	0.6	1.2	1.8	2.4
4	0.3	0.6	1.2	2.4	3.6	4.8
12	0.9	1.8	3.6	7.2	10.8	14.4
20	1.5	3.0	6.0	12.0	18.0	24.0
25	1.9	3.8	7.5	15.0	22.5	30.0
30	2.3	4.5	9.0	18.0	27.0	36.0
35	2.6	5.3	10.5	21.0	31.5	42.0
50	3.8	7.5	15.0	30.0	45.0	60.0

1% dilution = 6 drops or .3cc of catalyst per ounce of resin.
30cc = 1 ounce = 6 teaspoons = 600 drops

Glossary

BOW — The forward end of the boat.

BILGE AREAS - The curved portion of the hull between the relatively flat portions of the side and bottom.

COAMING — A raised border around a kayak cockpit. Used for attaching a spray skirt and for preventing water on the deck from running into the cockpit.

COCKPIT — The space in the kayak where the paddler sits. It is composed of a pad or seat on the bottom of the hull, a hole in the deck and a coaming around the hole.

DECK — The upper surface of a kayak extending from one sheer to the other. It stiffens the boat and prevents water from entering.

FOOTBALL — The long tapered area of the bottom in which the strips are straight and parallel to the keel, instead of curving around the middle of the boat from stem to stem.

FORMS — The plywood pattern pieces attached to the top of the strongback. They give the boat its shape while it is on the jig.

HULL — The water displacing surface of a kayak or canoe, extending from one sheer to the other.

KEEL — The strip of wood on the keel line projecting into the water from the hull. It assists the hull in gliding in a straight line.

KEEL LINE — The imaginary straight line running the length of the center of the bottom of the boat from one stem to the other.

PORTAGE — To carry the boat, often from one navigable water to another.

SCARF JOINT — A joining of two tapered pieces of wood by means of overlapping.

SHEER — The upper edges of the hull material extending from stem to stem. The gunnel of a canoe is attached there and the kayak hull is joined to the deck there.

SHIP—LAP — When the edge of one strip is raised above the adjoining strip. This is caused by twisting.

SPACER BLOCK — The wood blocks between the inwale and the sheer, in imitation of traditional gunnels which were assembled over the ends of ribs. They are fastened with glue and screws.

SPOKE SHAVE — A cutting blade set in a block that has two handles extending out to the sides so the tool can be drawn towards the operator. It is used to shave the edge of a curved piece of wood.

STEM — The apex or pointed end of a boat. Canoes and kayaks have a stem on each end.

STEM PIECE — The plywood pattern which defines the shape of the stem while the boat is on the jig.

STERN — The rear end of the boat

STRONGBACK — The backbone of a jig. A beam resting on legs for the purpose of holding the forms in alignment.

SURFORM TOOL — A combination rasp and plane made by Stanley, resembling a cheese grater and used for shaping.

THWARTS — Horizontal struts fastened to the gunnels for the purpose of stiffening the hull and maintaining its shape.

TRIM LINE — The calculated or indicated border of a piece of wood beyond which any material is in excess and will be cut or trimmed off.

TUMBLEHOME — Describes the sides of canoes whose sheer is narrower than their waterline, providing a greater bouyancy while maintaining a convenient reaching angle for the paddler.

Index

Feedback

This book began in 1972 as a 40 page opus de typewriter, reproduced on a newspaper format, with precious few illustrations. It was written mostly to answer the questions of people who wanted to build their own boat because they couldn't afford to buy the one I was building. In the following year, after discovering several improvements in technique, I began mailing out an addendum sheet of revisions with each copy, and finally in 1975 I published a much-expanded version of the newspaper. The second edition was saddle stitched with a cover and looked like a newsprint magazine with 86 pages. This third edition reflects the need for a more durable and attractive book and continues the expansion of material included. This edition has articles in the appendices on making canoe sails and your own paddle. In future editions I hope to include material on canvas covered canoes and kayaks, foam core fiberglass skinned boats, larger boats for sailing and fishing, and new information on resins and cloth. It is possible to extend related material indefinitely until the book becomes quite encyclopaedic in scope. You, the reader, can help me tremendously in this task by sending me feedback. Keep track of your expenses, your time, and your problems and solutions. Tell me about craftsmen who have knowledge worth sharing.

Following is a form you might want to use in writing to me. I look forward to hearing from you. THANK YOU.

David

Name

Address

Occupation(s); skills

Phone

Do you own a —

Canoe?   Kayak?   Row boat?   Other?

What brand?

Have you built any boats?

What kind?

How many?   How much did it cost?

How long did it take?

If you have built a wood strip boat did you do anything different from the way described in this book?

Why?

What did you do, in detail?

How well did it work?

What problems did you have?

Did you solve them?   How?

Do you have any technical ideas or resources to share?

In what way would you like to see this book improved or added to?

PLEASE DO NOT UNFOLD DRAWINGS UNTIL
THE BOOK IS PURCHASED